BUILDING AWESOME VACATIONS

The Legoland Book

Amy Bashor

Theme Park Press
The Happiest Books on Earth
www.ThemeParkPress.com

Editor: Bob McLain
Layout: Artisanal Text

ISBN 978-1-68390-223-2
Printed in the United States of America

Theme Park Press | www.ThemeParkPress.com
Address queries to bob@themeparkpress.com

Contents

Introduction

"Everything is awesome!" Once we watched the *Lego Movie*, it was impossible to get this song out of my head. My five year old sang it. My husband hummed it. I even found myself singing along while sitting on the floor building with Legos with my daughter. If there is a child in your house, I am willing to bet you know this song. I bet you have also played with Legos. Why? Because Legos really are awesome.

Our family may go overboard on the Lego enthusiasm. There are more than a dozen storage boxes of Legos, Duplos and other specialty brick systems in our home. My daughter takes her Lego creations to school to show her friends. My husband asks for Legos for holiday and birthday gifts. It is fair to say I am living with a couple of serious Lego fans.

Legoland seems like an obvious vacation destination for us. We travel to the Orlando area frequently for vacations. The thought of going to Legoland intrigued me for years. Yet I resisted actually booking a trip to check it out. I thought it was going to be a tiny little park we would finish in a few hours. And, well, to be blunt, I thought there was no possible way that Legoland would compare well to Walt Disney World.

After years of putting off a trip to Legoland, we finally decided to give it a try. One lovely morning in December 2015 we made our first visit to Legoland Florida. I was wrong about Legoland. It was far from the boring amusement park I had half expected. It is a vibrant park with plenty to appreciate. We have enjoyed several years of Legoland visits now and the park just keeps getting better. My sense is that this park is just starting to come into its own and will get even better over the next several years as the parent company of Legoland Florida, Merlin Entertainments, continues to invest in the park.

The simplicity of Legoland is part of what we enjoy about visiting this park. Legoland is easy. There is plenty to do, so no worries about getting bored in a small park. However, having a smaller set of choices reduces or eliminates the need to plan meals, rides and other attractions months in advance to get the best experience. Still, to be realistic, this park is always going to be the little brother of Disney, Universal and even SeaWorld. Legoland might best be viewed as a great compliment to other experiences in the Orlando area. It is a great weekend park.

In fact, you could easily walk into Legoland with nothing but this book and have a blast hitting the best of what the park has to offer. There is no need to make reservations for a place to stay a year in advance. No need to book meals at 180 days. No need to stay up till midnight 60 days prior to the trip to try to get the best Fast Pass. That's right, it is EASY to build an awesome vacation at Legoland Florida. Let's all take a collective sigh of relief. As a bonus, for those accustomed to Disney prices, not only is Legoland easy to plan and experience, it is relatively easy on the wallet.

So, if it is so easy, why should you keep reading this book? Well, mostly because it is a good way to get a real sense of what it is like to visit Legoland. There are relatively few sources of information on Legoland readily available. Reading will give you a good sense of how your family might enjoy a trip to Legoland. I will give you plenty of suggestions for how to make the most of a trip to the park. And since money always matters, we did several different trips at different budget levels. Reading this book will give you a way to walk through different experiences to get a feel for what might work best for your family. There are plenty of tips along the way on what we have learned about saving money at Legoland. And, for those who might want to indulge more, there are also thoughts on how to splurge a little for some meaningful extras that may make your family visit to Legoland even more awesome.

To be clear, I am not an insider. I do not work for Legoland. I am not associated with Legoland. I do not know any of their secrets. I am a theme park fan and a mom. I understand wanting to put together an awesome family vacation. I get that quality family vacation time is rare and valuable. I know just how much vacation time and money matter. I also know what it is like to plan a vacation and have nothing go as planned. This book will bring together all the things we did right.....any more importantly, all the things we did wrong, on multiple trips to Legoland. My hope is that sharing our experiences will help you make your Legoland vacation even more awesome!

CHAPTER ONE

Legoland Florida

Legoland in Florida is a fascinating theme park. This small park is expanding rapidly, with the full support of the second largest attractions operator in the world, Merlin Entertainments. Legoland's future builds on a rich past. This location was the site of one of the earliest parks in Florida, originally opened as a botanical garden in 1936. Today, Legoland Florida pays tribute to this history by maintaining part of this original botanical park as Cypress Gardens in the current park.

As I started learning more about the Legoland parks and Merlin Entertainments, I was startled to realize just how large a corporate family now owns the Legoland Park in Florida. While Disney is the most recognizable name in theme parks, Merlin is a bit of a sleeper. Under the Legoland brand alone, Merlin operates eight parks and nineteen Discovery Centers. Several disparate brands such as Legoland, SeaWorld, Madame Tussauds, and the Dungeons are part of the global organization that is Merlin.

Each brand targets a specific niche market. All of the Legoland parks and Discovery Centers are built for kids. These parks are intended, designed and built to appeal to young children. The Legoland Florida park is growing the meet the future in a way that stays very focused on the niche market it is built to serve: kids.

This book is written for that same niche market—families with young kids who will enjoy time at Legoland. The first chapter is structured somewhat like a traditional guide book to give an overview of the major lands and attractions at Legoland. It is a handy primer for the park, giving an overview of what this theme park can offer. It may also be useful to those thinking about which attractions will be of the most interest to family members. Subsequent chapters tell the story of our visits and showcase the different ways you can enjoy Legoland Florida.

Our family visited Legoland Florida many times over a three year period. We did quick day trips to Legoland while visiting Disney World, indulgent trips staying at the on-site Legoland Hotel and trips where we pinched pennies to squeeze in an extra vacation for some additional time at the park. We did a joint vacation with friends who have three young kids. We are planning a return visit in a few months for big extended family trip. It is these personal travel experiences at Legoland Florida that make up the heart of this book. We want to share what we learned over this trips to help your family have the awesomest family vacation.

Legoland is located in Winter Haven, which is about 45 minutes west of Orlando and about 45 minutes east of Tampa. The park is in the middle of the lake country of central Florida. There are some wonderful views, as Legoland is right on Lake Eloise. This is a theme park that is both old and new at the same time. The history of the park comes from its past as Cypress Gardens. Among other things, this means that Legoland benefits from absolutely lovely gardens as well as mature landscaping throughout the park. The new comes from the park's reinvention as Legoland and the continued investment in new attractions in the park since becoming Legoland. Together, this makes for a unique theme park experience.

We should go ahead and get to the bad news. Legoland is not in an ideal location for a tourist attraction. Getting to the park requires leaving the interstate and driving for at least twenty minutes into the country. Granted, the roads are nice highways with decent speed limits. Still, I simply can't see someone who is in Orlando for a convention driving by on the interstate and thinking "hey look, there's Legoland. I should go check it out." It is too far away for that type of impulsive visit. Location means Legoland will only get guests who are making the effort to travel to Winter Haven to get to the park.

The other key thing to know right from the beginning is that Legoland is not open every day of the calendar year. The Water Park closes for the winter. During these slower months, it is not unusual for the park to close completely a day or two during the week. If you are planning a visit to Legoland during these slower times of the year, please check the park website. There is a calendar there listing the days and times the park is open. One quick check can avoid the potential travel fiasco of arriving to play in the park on a day it is scheduled to be closed.

Legoland is located in Winter Haven Florida, which is mostly a sleepy little town. It has a few hotels, some chain stores and a water ski museum. However, there are several restaurants. The area has just about every chain restaurant available plus some unique local eateries. For example, there is a sweet store that serves goat milk fudge, which sounds cooler than it tastes. This is located on the primary route from I-4 to Legoland.

There are two exits off I-4 that lead to the park. Both are easy drives. Driving from Orlando, exit 55 is the first option. This route is a fairly very direct path to Legoland on Highway 27. There are plenty of fast food options on this route for dining as well as some fairly typical strip mall shopping options. On the other hand, driving just a bit further and leaving I-4 on exit 48 allows for a bit more nostalgic drive. This scenic drive winds through the country, including passing some orange tree groves, as well as some of the older sections of Winter Haven.

I prefer the exit 48 route. This is an interesting drive. Some of the sights include a number of old school fast food signs at locations that look like they have been around for decades. The first time, we missed exit 55 and wound up going this way by accident. On return trips, I have taken it just to enjoy the sights. Seeing the orange groves in particular is a sharp reminder of some road trips with my family when I was a little girl. It is a nice way to mentally slow down and relax to enjoy a day or two at Legoland.

In the end, both routes lead to the main entrance of Legoland. You turn in and follow the curving road around to the toll booths. Yes, much like other theme parks, the lines start before you even leave the car. At the parking lot toll booth, you have the option of paying for regular or for preferred parking for the day. There are three ways to avoid paying for parking.

The first way to avoid the parking fee is not to park at Legoland. This is simpler than it might seem, as there are several local chain hotels referred to as "Brick and Bed" partners that offer free shuttle services to the park from the hotel and back again in the afternoon. There are also shuttle services that connect the Merlin Entertainment options on International Drive to Legoland. The second way is to stay at the Legoland hotel. This is an expensive way to save money. The Legoland hotel offers more for families than local chain hotels and the rates reflect that with a significantly increased cost.

The third way to avoid the parking toll is to purchase an annual pass. One of the benefits of an annual pass for Legoland is free parking at the park. However, the parking fee is only waived after you have the annual pass. This means that if you upgrade to the annual pass while visiting the park, you will have to pay parking on that first visit. I made this mistake and was annoyed there was no way to get reimbursed for that initial parking fee when I upgraded. Almost two years later, we purchased another annual pass while at the iDrive 360 complex in Orlando. This gave us the parking free the first time we visited Legoland after purchasing that annual pass.

There are two different fees for parking. The lower cost option is for parking in the regular lots. For a slight additional cost, there is also preferred parking spots. The regular parking was just fine when we first starting visiting the park. However, once Legoland rolled out an upgraded preferred parking area that include better spots closer to the gate and covered parking, we converted to preferred parking. As a nice bonus, the parking cover is topped with solar panels.

Before we even enter the park built for kids, the parking lot provides a nice educational moment. My daughter gets a kick out of talking about solar energy when we park. We talk about the benefits and drawbacks of solar power and usually wind up giggling about the irony of the planet's ultimate heat source providing a cooler place for our car to park in the hot Florida sun. This is worth the slight upcharge to me. That said, paying for preferred parking is just that, a personal preference. There is plentiful parking, and even the furthest parking spots are a reasonable walking distance. There is no need for a parking tram in the Legoland lot.

In both the regular and the preferred parking spots, the different parking areas are identified by Lego characters. While the parking lot is not enormous, it is certainly large enough someone in the family needs to remember where you parked. Referencing the parking areas by the Lego characters is an easy way to do make it easy to remember.

Once parked, grab your gear and head for the park entrance. You will notice the Legoland hotel as you walk to the park entrance. Just walk that way – the hotel is located right beside the park entrance. As you get close to the ticket area with the huge Legoland sign, you will be greeted by the now ubiquitous bag check and metal detection security stop. Knowing this is coming is helpful, as you can then plan to take easy open bags for the line. Security checks tend to more fairly quickly at Legoland.

On the other hand, the ticket booths tend to be the opposite of fast. When I've stopped to pay attention, it is almost like watching the DMV scene from Zootopia. You may feel differently, but I don't want to send my limited vacation time waiting in line to buy tickets. Instead, it is easy to buy tickets ahead of time either on the Legoland site or some other online sales option. One of the simplest ways to check for reputable ways to buy tickets online is to check the mousesavers website, which does a good job of keeping updated information on discount tickets posted.

Ticket in hand, the next step is the actual turnstile to scan the ticket and walk into the park. If you happen to get to this point about fifteen minutes or so before the park is scheduled to open, there is a short welcome show with a Lego character. Being picked as the family to help open the park might be fun. Otherwise, I'd suggest skipping this show. It puts you right in the middle of the opening crowd. If there is a way to zig when the crowd zags at a theme park, it will almost always save you time and aggravation. The annual pass is helpful for this at park opening. It allows passholders to enter the park 30 minutes before the official opening time.

Once inside the park, there are a number of themed areas. Some of these lands are going to appeal more to different age groups than others. Or perhaps I should say some of these lands are going to appeal more to some kids more than others. My daughter is not a thrill seeker, so she tends to prefer the areas designed more for the younger kids. On the other hand, our nephews are totally about the rush. They want to beeline for the roller coasters every time. Knowing what to find in which area of the park helps us get everyone where they want to go.

Plus, since I like to sneak in every chance I can to make learning full, one of the things we do before a trip is spend some time looking at maps. Samantha started learning to read maps by visiting theme parks. You can download a PDF of the current park map from the Legoland website. Printing that map might help visualize how the lands in the park are laid out.

THE BEGINNING

Logically enough, the first area inside the park is called The Beginning. As you enter, there are large Lego sculptures that immediately catch the eye. It's best to be cautious when walking through, as occasionally water will shoot out of these to wake up the unwary. Over to the left as you walk in are the guest service areas for stroller/wheelchair rentals, lockers, package pickup and photo pick up.

This is also the area for Lost Parents. Children are never lost in Legoland, but parents can get temporarily misplaced. Discuss this with your kids ahead of time to make sure they know what to do if needed. We drill our daughter on our names, telephone numbers and safe adults. At Legoland, the safe adults are the Model Citizens. That's the park term for employees. Model Citizens are easily identified by their name tags, which are small Lego plates and include at least one mini-figure. Samantha knows these Model Citizens will help her find us if we happen to get separated. While that has never happened, better safe than sorry. Walking past this area usually prompts me to double check and make sure my daughter is still clear on these details.

The Big Shop, which is one of the larger stores in the park, is in the Beginning. This is usually our last stop on the way out of the park. So far, we have not made it out yet without buying sometime. If you want to keep unplanned Lego purchases out of the budget, avoid this store. Actually, avoid all the stores if the plan is not to buy Legos. There are so many tempting sets that walking out without any is going to be an exercise in extreme self-control for Lego fans.

The Beginning also has the coffee shop, a milkshake shop and one of the larger restaurants. These are fairly standard fare for any theme park or family attraction. They feature okay food at inflated prices. If you have recently purchased popcorn at almost any movie theater in America, you have a good idea of the price inflation phenomenon.

Sadly, the one ride in the Beginning, named the Island in the Sky, closed permanently in 2018. This is unfortunate, as it was one of our favorite rides in the park. It wa a legacy ride, with more than thirty years of history dating back to the prior theme parks located on the same grounds. A rotating platform on a large crane arm gently lifted guests 150 feet in the air for a nice view of the park and surrounding areas. This was a slow and easy ride, well suited for just about anyone.

I am going to keep my fingers crossed that perhaps something will happen and Legoland will find a way to bring this ride back at some point in the future.

FUN TOWN

Once past the Beginning, the next area of the park is called Fun Town. This functions somewhat like a hub for the park, as you can head in three different directions for three different lands from Fun Town. There is one ride in Fun Town, the Grand Carousel. This ride is the centerpiece of the area and is a highly effective magnet for the youngest kids. It is a double decker carousel fitted with child size Duplo horse replicas.

There is no easy way to avoid the carousel. Go ahead and prepare yourself for a wait in line. The ride has relatively few seats and takes a while to load. And it is a good bet that the youngest kids in your party are going to want to ride it. There is no minimum height for the Grand Carousel, although riders under 48 inches tall have to be accompanied. And if you are traveling with a young girl, it might be worth your time to scout out the nearest white horse. For some reason, it seems every other young girl wants to ride one of the white horses. There are not that many on the carousel. I can recall at least twice asking the Model Citizen working the ride if we could stand aside to let others past us so my daughter could have first pick of the horses to get the one she wanted. This is a useful way to ask for a preferred position for almost any theme park ride, although it does means more wait time to get what we want. I'm okay with that.

Fun Town also plays host to stores and places to eat. The most unique is Granny's Apple Fries. Think apples sliced, fried and dipped in caramel or whipped cream. That is what is sold here. It sounds like it should be absolutely fantastic. It is okay and well worth trying once. I didn't care for it all that much, at least not until we decided to add ice cream. That is a combination worth trying. There is also Fun Town Slushies, a classic carnival drink.

One place we enjoy eating in Fun Town is the Pizza and Pasta Buffet. If there are big eaters in the family, that is where I would head for lunch. The buffet includes unlimited salad bar with multiple pizza, pasta and bread options. As usual in a theme park, the shortest waits and lowest crowds for any restaurant are going to be before or after the typical lunch rush.

Stores in Fun Town include the Lego Pick A Brick Factory store, which has a wall of loose Legos for sale in addition to the Lego sets and other themed items. This is also the home of the Studio Store and the Mini-figure Market. Samantha enjoyed making mini-figures here. They are sold primarily in sets of three for around $10. If your child likes mini-figures, it will take some time to get them out of this store.

Across from the Factory store is the Studio Store. This is the place to pick up TV and movie themed Lego products. A good tip for the different stores inside Legoland is to ask to have your purchases transferred to the Big Store in the Beginning for package pickup. That is much simpler than carrying around boxes all day.

Fun Town hosts the Wells Fargo Fun Town 4D Town Theater. The show selection rotates to keep up with the latest in the world of animated Legos. In one of the shows, the stars of the Lego Movie reunite for a trip to a park that is not quite Legoland. This is a fun show that fans of the movie will enjoy. The movie has a slow start, which may displease the younger members of the audience. However, things picked up quickly and went well. My guess is that if a family member enjoyed the Lego Movie, they will like the Lego Movie 4D. Just prepare to get a little windblown and/or damp from the 4D effects.

The 700-seat Wells Fargo Fun Town Theater also features other shows, which have included the Legends of Chima and a Clutch Powers Adventure. These shows link back to different rides or areas in the Legoland park, making them a nice accompaniment to the rides. These characters also tend to link back to Lego shows or movies. My daughter did some searching to find Clutch Powers and watch it after we saw these characters at the Legoland movie theater. Because the movies do vary to stay current, the best bet is to pick up a copy of the show times guide when you enter the park. It will list the movie times for the day.

Another way to maximize the kids enjoyment of the Legoland park might be to look for some of these shows ahead of time. Netflix has been a good source for these shows. Although the line up changes, we have found Ninjago, Clutch Powers and a few other Lego shows there. Checking out a couple of these ahead of time should give a reasonable indication for how much the kids might enjoy watching the show in the theater.

DUPLO VALLEY

As Legoland is the park for kids, Duplo Valley is the land for the youngest kids. This area almost always winds up being our next stop after a ride on the carousel. Even now, my daughter still loves the rides in this land. It is the only theme park land where she can ride every ride by herself. Of course, she still prefers Daddy or me to come along with her, but the option is there when she's ready. If your preschooler is pushing for a little more independence, this might be a good way to let them have the experience of doing a ride on their own for the first time.

On the other hand, if your kids have passed into grade school, it may be worth walking past Duplo Valley. These rides tend to be low capacity, with relatively long loading and unloading times. Together, this means more time waiting in line than riding rides.

Walking into Duplo Valley from Fun Town, the Duple Tractor ride will fascinate kids. There are several buttons to push near the fence that surrounds the ride that make animal noises. While I do not understand why this fascinates young children so much, they seem to love it. Once you get them past this fun, they might notice the big barn directly opposite the tractor. More formally known as the Duplo Farm, this place is a magnet for kids. Ours has been known to spend over an hour happily playing in here. It might be worth highlighting this next point. The Duplo Farm building is air conditioned and has seats for parents.

The Duplo Farm is a climate controlled haven on hot days. The inside is a large room with several different Lego themed play areas. One play structure looks like a two story house, with room to play on the bottom and a slide coming off the second floor. Another play area looks like the barn, complete with a large Duplo chicken standing on the roof. This has a larger slide as well as a first story play area. There are a couple of other smaller play structures. Each has containers of Duplo blocks. It is easy to spend a lot of time in the Barn if you have young kids.

Tucked in the back corner behind the play equipment is the Baby Care Center. This is a sanctuary for parents, especially nursing moms, with infants. It is important to note that only babies are welcome in this Baby Care Center. Unlike other parks, there are not toddler friendly toilets available for the preschool set. Instead, take a small post-it pad if automatic toilets scare your little ones. This is an easy way to fool the sensor and allow the child to finish their business in peace. Actually, keeping post-it's in a purse for this purpose all the time might not be a bad idea.

The Baby Care Center in the Barn is by far the nicest baby care center of any theme park I have personally visited. There are multiple small private rooms for moms to nurse or feed their babies. The entire area was sparkling clean and quiet, including the diaper changing stations. This is a great place to take baby when either parent or child needs a little time to chill.

When you emerge from the Barn, you will see one more toddler sized ride and a several play areas. The second ride is the Duplo Train. Much like the Tractor ride, it is a fairly typical amusement park kiddie ride. The Train is themed to show off Duplo blocks. Kids will love the rides. Parents may be less than thrilled with the smaller sized seats on the Train. If your child is ready to try going for a solo ride, this may be one where it makes sense to wait in line with them, then wave them farewell and take photos while they enjoy their ride.

There is a Tot Spot play area, complete with miniaturized play equipment and very large blocks, in Duplo Valley. The Tot Spot is shaded, which is a considerate touch for the Florida heat. Other play options include a Splash & Play. There is an automated dryer by the play area. It may be scary to some young kids. If you child is going to want to get wet playing, packing an extra dry outfit or two might be the best plan. Actually, packing some dry clothes is a good plan for kids in theme parks. If not wet, someone will end up dirty, sticky or otherwise disheveled.

During the Christmas season, Duple Valley plays host to different holiday activities. You might find Mrs. Clause reading Christmas stories. Or you might color a Lego themed Christmas card for the big guy. There is usually a large Lego Christmas display in this area for the season. We had fun taking pictures in a Lego sleigh here one year.

There are no stores or restaurants in Duplo Valley. This place is all about the little kids. Yes, that means your older kids may be bored silly with the available play areas and rides. If you have older and younger children in the group, dividing and conquering may be a good plan. Most little kids are going to love it here and may not want to move on to explore the rest of the park.

WORLD OF CHIMA BECOMES LEGO MOVIE WORLD

A new land opened in Legoland Florida in 2019. The Lego Movie and the Lego Movie 2 have proved popular with fans. This content is an ideal fit for Legoland. In fact, characters from the Lego Movie started showing up in Legoland in an exclusive movie at the theater, in character meets and in other small ways throughout the park back when the first Lego Movie came out. Now, characters from the Lego Movies have their own land, simply named Lego Movie World.

This new land features three rides, character meet-and-greets, food stand and a play area. It is designed to feel as if you are standing in Bricksburg from a child's perspective. Sorry, Chima fans, but I think the park made the right call with this move. Not only does the move add additional rides and activities to the park, this is a land that can grow with the park. If additional movies are made, it is easy to see how new characters and story lines could keep this land fresh and interesting.

Before it closed, the World of Chima was based on a line of Lego toys released in 2013. Eight different animal tribes are at war in a fantasy environment to find magical crystals called Chi. These are basically the power source for the kingdom. This small land was one ride, an associated water play area for the little ones and one shopping area. The ride, the Quest for Chi, was a water boat ride designed to give lots of opportunities to soak others.

Fans of the Quest for Chi water ride will recognize many familiar elements in Battle for Bricksburg. Riders board boats and use the on-board water canons to fight off alien Duplo invaders. Of course, what innocent unsuspecting riders may not know is that other park guests, like my husband, can find other water cannons mounted around the perimeter of the ride to help fight back. One way or another, guests on the Battle for Bricksburg should prepare to get wet.

The second ride in Bricksburg is named Masters of Flight. This ride is Legoland's response to motion simulator rides in other parks, with the unique Lego twist. It seems that Emmett, who you may remember from the Lego Movies, has entered a contest for Master Builders. His entry is a Triple Decker Flying Couch. How awesome is that? I think fans of Soarin' at Disney are going to really enjoy the Triple Decker Flying Couch. And even if you happen not to like the ride, which I find unlikely, fans of the movie are going to enjoy seeing the building that houses the ride. It is designed to look like the puppy head where the Lego heroes meet.

Emmett takes guests along for a ride through Cloud Cuckoo Land and other spaces that will look familiar to fans of the films. Rather than being lifting into the air, the ride vehicle makes a turn into the action. The marketing for the ride calls it out as specifically choreographed to make guests feel like they are really flying in the Triple Decker Couch. I think this ride would be an awesome way to introduce young kids to these types of rides. Perhaps I should give the disclaimer that these are among my very favorite rides, so I may be biased to liking this ride.

There is a second brand new ride in this land, Unikitty's Disco Drop. One of the more intriguing

characters from the Lego Movies is Unikitty. This
Duplo character goes through moods faster than my
daughter goes through clothes on vacation. That wildly
changing emotional climate is reflected in a tower ride
that brings guests up into the air to experience Cloud
Cuckoo Land before bouncing and twisting down in
an abrupt change of mood. Young adventure seekers
should enjoy this ride. Actually, adults might enjoy
this one as well. The seats are comfortable for adults
and there is a chance to catch air a couple of times on
the ride. Much like the Triple Decker Couch, the Disco
Drop is designed for kids and fun for the family.

My daughter loves play areas. The new play area
in the Lego Movie World land is nicely themed as
Benny's Spaceship. This relatively small play area is
several stories, with both a large and small twisty
slide and landing decks for play. This is one of the few
misses in the land in my opinion. A larger play area
here with nearby seating for parents might have been
a better option.

When Legoland added the Lego Friends land a few
years ago, they included a specific character meeting
area. That must have worked well, as it was repeated
in Lego Movie Land. Emmett has his own suite, which
serves as a dedicated character meet area. Right next
to this meet area is the Awesome Shop, giving guests
another opportunity to load up on Legos and other toys.

Rounding out the new land is the Taco Everyday
stand. This fast food restaurant has a few different
taco options and includes a distinctly adult option
with beer on the menu for parents. Perhaps my favorite thing here is the shaded area with tables.

Transitioning the World of Chima to the Lego
Movie World was a smart decision. The land will be
much more recognizable to the majority of guests and
the rides should be a nice transition from the toddler

rides of Duplo to the more thrilling roller coaster options in the other lands. If you or your kids enjoyed either of the Lego Movies, give this land a try.

LEGO KINGDOMS

The next land, Lego Kingdoms, has several attractions to offer. There is something for everyone in the family here. While not technically listed as an attraction, the Lego castle in this area deserves mention. If you catch the park during a slow time, this is fantastic photo opportunity area. During one visit to Legoland, my daughter was still in her princess dress and fancy hair from a makeover at Disney World. She quite liked being the only princess in the castle and happily posed for pictures here.

Lego Kingdoms has a roller coaster. The Dragon is a legacy ride from the Cypress Gardens period of the park's history. It was open from 2004 to 2008, when it was called Okeechobee Rampage. When Legoland opened, the ride was repurposed to be the Dragon to fit the theme of Lego Kingdoms. It combines a short dark ride featuring Lego Kingdom figures with a relatively tame coaster ride, topping out at 28 miles per hour. The total ride is about two minutes long.

Across the courtyard from the entrance to the Dragon, a covered carnival type ride, is available for the littlest kids and likely only appealing to them. The entire ride is approximately the size of a large gazebo. The ride vehicles travel in a circle with gentle ups and downs right where parents can watch the entire ride. My favorite element of this ride is the Lego book here that begins "Once Upon A Time."

The Royal Joust is just for kids. I didn't pay attention to the signs or the park map that clearly express this. Instead, I waited in the queue to ride only to be told "Sorry, Mom, this one is for the children." Rats!

My daughter was not entirely certain about riding by herself at first, then decided to give it a go. Three repeat rides later, it was fairly clear this ride was a hit. Kids ride Lego horses around a track full of different Lego figures. Although the characters are human, the look and feel of this ride very much reminds me of the animated Disney movie Robin Hood. Kids must be 36 inches or taller and 12 years of age or younger to ride the Royal Joust.

Directly across from the Royal Joust is the largest play area, the Forestmen's Hideout. This area has several different types of play structures. There are many climbing options, which makes this a wonderful area to bring restless kids who need to run around and burn off some energy. It is also a nice shady spot for anyone looking for a cooler option in the Florida afternoon sun. The biggest challenge we have faced here is getting our daughter out to continue exploring the park.

There is also a fast food burger option here – the Castle Burger. There are a few tables in the vicinity and a small stage. During the Christmas season, there are live shows on this stage. The show tends to be funny, with an emphasis on physical humor appropriate to all ages. If there are no shows, this is a good spot to take a short break.

Lego Kingdoms also has its own shopping option called the King's Market. In addition, there are characters made of Legos scattered about, carnival style games to be played at an additional cost and face painters lying in wait. It may be best to decide ahead of time if you are willing to budget for these additional park expenses. Unplanned indulging can add unanticipated costs fairly quickly.

As you exit Lego Kingdoms, there are two options for moving on to other areas. Continuing straight ahead takes you to the Land of Adventure. The other choice is to hang a sharp left and head towards

Miniland USA. We usually head to Land of Adventure, as that area has another ride favorite for our family.

LAND OF ADVENTURE

The Land of Adventure is home to five attractions, plus carnival games and two snack cart type food options. This area is loosely themed to the adventures of Clutch Powers, a Lego version of an adventurer who reminds me very much of Indiana Jones. Walking into the Land of Adventure from Lego Kingdoms, you will walk past several carnival games on the left. On the other side of the games is one of my favorite rides in the Legoland park, the Lost Kingdom Adventure.

The Lost Kingdom Adventure features mummies and other Egyptian design. This dark ride is a first person shooter. The goal is to use your on-board gun to shoot as many targets as possible in the ride to rack up points. Also I think maybe you save a Lego character from another character, but I've never been clear on that aspect. This is a family friendly ride, with a minimum height requirement of 34 inches.

The Lost Kingdom Adventure is the same kind of ride as Buzz Lightyear Space Ranger Spin, the Toy Story Midway Mania or the Men in Black ride. However, the theming for this ride is nowhere near the level of the Disney or Universal rides. Expect a more basic experience that is much less immersive. That said, the Lost Kingdom Adventure is one we do every time we visit the park and always enjoy. The characters and interactive elements of the ride are fun if basic.

Just outside the Lost Kingdom Adventure is a carnival type bounce ride named the Beetle Bounce. This is a very straight forward up and down ride that is over very quickly. I have yet to get my daughter to try this ride as she says it looks scary. It is not scary. In fact, it may well be too tame for any true thrill seekers in the family.

Tucked in a corner of the courtyard in front of the Lost Kingdom Adventure is the play area called Pharaoh's Revenge. This is my daughter's favorite play area. It may look like just another covered play area from the outside. We skipped this one for several visits. Don't let the outside fool you. Inside, this place is more active than seems possible from its quiet facade. There are air powered ball guns. Kids take gleeful pride is seeing how many people they can shoot. Parents, enter at your own risk. Samantha absolutely loves this play area. She would spend hours in here if we let her.

Carnival games, face painting and other additional cost activities are throughout the Land of Adventure. There is an element of this area that feels like a state fair or regional amusement park to me. I would be shocked to see a child make it all the way through this far into the park without asking their adult for some money to play one of these games.

The Land of Adventure is home to two additional rides. Walking on, the Safari Trek on the left is squarely aimed at younger kids. My daughter would love to ride this more often, but the seats in the little cars were not comfortable for us adults. My husband and I might have played rock-paper-scissors to determine who went with her on this ride. As the exit is right beside the entrance, it may be that this is one ride the kids would be okay doing on their own.

However, it is well worth squeezing into the ride vehicles at Safari Trek at least once. The Lego animals are really a treat for anyone who loves Legos. Large Lego Elephants squirt water out of their trunks, giraffe reach for leaves, a lion family perches on their rocks and there are several other little surprises along the way. The whole ride is typically less than three minutes, which means most days you will spend more time waiting in line than on this ride. Much like the

Royal Joust, this is a ride my daughter loves and will do several times when visiting Legoland.

Across from the Sarafi Trek, the thrill seekers encounter their first serious looking coaster. The Coastersaurus roller coaster is one of the most interesting rides in the park. Between the original Cypress Gardens, which started as a botanical garden and Legoland, there were a couple of unsuccessful attempts to run amusement parks here. The Coastersaurus is a rebranded ride from the amusement park that immediately preceded Legoland, the Cypress Garden Adventure Park. This roller coaster opened originally in November 2004, when it was named the Triple Hurricane for the three hurricanes that threatened Florida that year.

With a ride time of just under a minute and a top speed of 32 miles per hour, this little coaster might just be the perfect introduction to the world of wooden roller coasters. In the Legoland incarnation, the Coastersaurus has been mostly updated with the addition of Lego dinosaurs. Guests 42 inches to 48 inches may ride accompanied by an adult and guests over 48 inches tall may ride by themselves. Outside the coaster is one of my favorite photo opportunities in the parks, with a large dinosaur tucked to the side to welcome guests. This area has both shade and fewer crowds than the dinosaurs out front, both big advantages for photos in my opinion.

LEGO NINJAGO WORLD

The Lego brand has a significant hit with the Ninjago series. My daughter, her cousins, friends and casual acquaintances all somehow seem to know the story of these ninja style characters learning fancy moves to defeat a bewildering array of bad guys. I like that there is a strong female character and a few decent life lessons in the series. Mostly, though, this is campy good fun for parents and kids.

The Lego Ninjago World is a really well done area. The theming is outstanding. In my opinion, this is the most immersive area in the park. Again, it is just an opinion, but I think the dark ride that is the main attraction at Lego Ninjago stands up well to Midway Mania in Disney's Hollywood Studios Toy Story land. The area outside the ride is also really well themed and has a really fun play area with a storyline for kids. My only disappointment in this land is that it is so small. With Coastersaurus on one side and the City Stage on the other, I don't see much room for this land to expand. That's really too bad.

The area in front of the ride has several intricate buildings, characters and dragons made of course of Legos. Master Wu himself—at least his child sized, Lego version—stands near the front of the area to welcome you. He points to a sign with imaginative names for the play area in the courtyard of the ride. Kids can check out Zane's Temple Build then try to make it through Kai's Spinners, Jay's Lighting Drill and Cole's Rock Climb before getting to the ride building. We spend more time in this play area than on the ride, as my daughter really enjoys the challenges here. There are easily scaled so kids can make this easier or harder for themselves, which means Samantha can keep challenging herself on the same course on repeat visits.

Inside the Lego Ninjago World is one of the newest additions to Legoland Florida. This ride opened at the Florida park in January 2017 following its debut at the California park in 2016. However, it may be the coolest ride at Legoland. I love dark rides where I can shoot things. The Ninjago ride kicks that coolness factor up a notch, because this ride doesn't use a gun. Instead, you master the spinjitzu moves while walking the queue and use your hands to take out targets on the ride.

If the Ninjago land were the size and scope of the Lego Movie Land, I think this would be the most popular area of the park. Happily, the one ride is extremely well done and has the capacity to handle the crowds. Occasionally, the park will offer special Ninjago days with additional characters, builds and challenges for guests. If anyone in the family is especially devoted to the art of spinjitzu, trying to time a visit for one of these Ninjago days might be fun.

LEGO CITY

Continuing past Ninjago World is perhaps the most ride-dense section of the park, Lego city. The Lego City area has a roller coaster, boat ride, two little car rides and an interesting fire engine ride that requires physical engagement. There are also great photo opportunities here with a full size car made of Legos and smaller replicas for children to play in while waiting. There are three food options in Lego City and a store. It is also the gateway to the water park.

Walking in from Ninjago World, the first attraction guests will see is the Boating School. This is a fun boat ride that gives guests control of the little boats. We try to catch this attraction during slow times. My daughter really likes this ride. However, it is another low capacity, slow loading ride. Also, the typical requirement for this ride is three people to a boat. That works well for kids. It works less well for adults. That means trying for this ride at slower times when I feel comfortable asking for two boats for the three of us. Or, it means I may opt to hang back and take pictures while my husband and daughter ride. This is a good ride for photos, as non-riders have plenty of room to stand with a great view and the boats just don't move that fast.

The boats meander around a canal under the control of the pilot. This gives kids a chance to actually drive the boat. My daughter loved this freedom, which incidentally also means this is a slow ride. Frankly, this can be a boring ride for the adult in the boat. I found counting the Lego themed surprises throughout the ride to be an entertaining distraction. Kids 34 inches or taller can ride with adults and children 48 inches or taller can go alone. Sending the taller kids off on their own would be a good way to get good photos or videos of them enjoying this ride.

Next up are the Driving School attractions. There are two of these, one for the younger set who are younger than six years old and one for the bigger kids who have passed their sixth birthday. These are little cars, shaped to look like Lego cars, that the kids free drive on tracks. The tracks are cute, the cars are cute and this is a fantastic place to get some cute photos.

Kids who do either Driving School get a little card after completing the ride. The younger set get a generic card, where parents can fill in the name and date. Big kids can either get a similar generic cards, or parents can then take the kids and card to a building in the area to get a Lego Driver's License printed for their child. While this comes at a slight additional cost, it may be a fun memento of the trip.

Active parents who would like to pump a fire engine or police car on something resembling a train track may enjoy doing the NFPA Rescue Academy with their kids. This is a multi-step, group activity ride. First, families are assigned a rescue vehicle and get onboard. Next, they use an old fashioned human powered pump to move the vehicle. This propels the family on the vehicle down the track to the scene of the fire.

Once there, the adults continue the arm exercise by pumping a fire hydrant to put out a pretend fire before getting back in their vehicles. Then parents pump the vehicle to power it back to the starting line.

While technically kids 48 inches and taller go can go on the Rescue Academy by themselves, that just seems cruel. As kids only need to be 36 inches to go with an adult, know before you go if you are willing to do this ride. It can be a ton of fun. It is certainly much more of a work out than you might expect to get from a theme park ride.

The final attraction in Lego City is the Flying School. Kids must be 44 inches to ride with an adult or 52 inches to go by themselves. This is an inverted roller coaster. Riders sit with their legs suspended to add to the feeling of flying while they are strapped in with a safety harness. This is one of the legacy rides in the park from prior to the Legoland purchase. The coaster was first called Swamp Thing, it was originally built for Cypress Gardens. It has been one of the main hits of the park since it opened and continues to be very popular as a rethemed Lego ride.

Flying School starts with a five story climb. It goes quickly through the twists and drops of the track, finishing the track in less than two minutes at a top speed of 25 miles per hour. Because it is one of the more thrilling rides in the park, the wait can get long here on busy days. Happily, there is an air conditioned play area just outside the queue entrance for the coaster for younger siblings to play on soft flying themed play equipment while the big girls and boys get their flying lesson on the coaster.

There are three options for food in Lego City. It is hard to go wrong with ice cream, which makes Firehouse Ice Cream a favorite stop here. The brick option is a personal favorite and is plenty big enough for three to share. I once sent my family on to the Imagination Zone so I could surprise them with a brick of ice cream for us to share. This ice cream option includes many scoops and toppings. I am not sure how any one person could finish one of these but the three of us enjoyed sharing most of one before giving up on finishing all of it.

The burgers at the Lego City Burger Kitchen are somewhere between McDonalds and Five Guys quality. They are decent. However, for not much more cost, the Fun Town Pizza and Pasta Buffet is a better bet for anyone feeding teenage boys or others with hollow legs.

The Fried Chicken Company gives another option for those who can't face another theme park burger. Again, it is more or less typical theme park quality food. It will fill you up if you are in the mood for chicken.

If any of the Lego City attractions sound like they will be favorites for your kids, it might be best to start the day back here. These rides are popular and that means lines can start backing up fairly quickly. Families and school groups visiting for the first time are more likely to start towards the front of the park, but you can zip on back for these rides to enjoy them before the crowds arrive.

IMAGINATION ZONE

Walking back from Lego City leads first to the Imagination Zone. Attractions here include the Imagination Pavilion, Kid Power Towers, Lego MindStorms and a panini shop. The outdoor art seems designed to spark the imagination, as it includes a giant Lego Einstein head and a giant giraffe. The I-Zone Panini shop feature hot sandwiches and good salads.

The Kid Power Tower is the sole ride in this area of the park. While it is technically a ride, calling it such is a bit of a stretch. This is really more of a controlled fall. Kids must be at least 38 inches to give it a solo try and kids under 48 inches must be accompanied by an adult. The ride seats are connected to short towers. Once secured in the ride seat, riders pull themselves up to the top of the tower before being dropped back down again. Much like the rescue ride in Lego City, adults seem to provide most of the ride power. Thus, the name of the ride—Kid Power Tower—seems amusingly ironic.

As part of the ongoing work to enhance Legoland, the Imagination Pavilion was closed for a renovation in 2015 and reopened in the summer of 2016. It is now better than ever. It features distinct zones within the building. These include the Creation Zone, Water Zone, Wheels Zone, Building Zone and Flight Zone. It is an indoor, climate controlled area. This by itself would ensure popularity during some months of the year.

Now add to that some of the best aspects of the Legoland hotel. There are pits of Legos for kids to play with. There are large tables set up with buildings that can be used for play as-is or as a launch point to continue creating the town. You can race wheeled Lego creations and flight test those with wings. There is a shake table to test your creations ability to resist an earthquake. And if all that is not enough, the new virtual Lego aquarium in the Imagination Pavilion is fantastic fun.

The ability to build and test Lego creations is a great deal of fun. Each zone allows for specific testing. For example, in the Flight Zone, there are miniature zip lines for guests to send their creations flying. As one of the Model Citizens told me, most of these wind up crashing, which is typically just more encouragement to go build again. The race zone is somewhat like the race tables outside the Lego store in Disney Springs, only more elaborate. The track looks more like a race track and the walls extend the theme. As a hands-on creation area where guests can build their own Lego models and test them, the Imagination Pavilion is a clear win for keeping little hands busy and out of trouble.

In the Game Zone, guests are invited to play the latest Lego themed video games. It may be best not to let any dedicated gamers in the family to find their way into this building. Non gamers will likely find this space a yawn and be eager to move on to the next thing.

Budding engineers and armchair engineers alike will get a kick out of MindStorms. Here, guests get to build and program robots. One caveat—this activity may not be available to large groups like school groups. MindStorms also requires signing up for it and spaces are limited.

Lego Master Builders in training may well want to skip the rest of the park and head directly here to the Imagination Zone. The different building and testing options are a ton of fun. The challenge of MindStorms gives older kids who may not be thrilled with the kiddie rides in the park a change to really stretch their minds and their imaginations.

CYPRESS GARDENS

The most historic part of Legoland is the legacy land-scaping known as Cypress Gardens. Go ahead and skip ahead to chapter nine if you want to dig into the history of the parks that preceded Legoland in Winter Haven. It is a fascinating story of the founder living out the American dream, the hard times that can bedevil any business and the eventual resurrection of Cypress Gardens as Legoland.

In today's Legoland park, Cypress Gardens is a showpiece that includes nods to its historic past with features such as Southern Belles made of Lego bricks in its current configuration. As a themed area in Legoland, Cypress Gardens features wide walking paths through grassy glades, a lovely gazebo with a Lego Southern Belle, a large banyan tree, views of Lake Eloise, bridges over the old canals, the pool shaped like the state of Florida and many different plants and flowers from around the world. It is an oasis of peace and quiet.

As the signs clearly indicate, there is wildlife present in the Gardens. Well, it is Florida. If there is a standing body of water, assume alligators are present and act accordingly by staying out of the water. Snakes are also a real possibility, as are spiders. However, the Gardens get a fair amount of human traffic every day. Taking sensible precautions like looking at the ground where you are walking and staying on the designated walking paths should be all that is needed for a safe adventure exploring in the Gardens.

The Gardens are open to visitors of all ages. They are a serene counterpart to the energy and excitement of the rest of the park. Be aware the Gardens tend to close earlier than the rest of the lands in the park. A good time to visit here is after lunch, when the sun is at its height and some shade sounds like a good idea to everyone in the family.

LEGO TECHNIC

The more adventurous members of the family may drift towards the Lego Technic area. It plays host to both a roller coaster, once called Project X and now rethemed into a VR roller coaster called the Great Lego Race, and a water ride, Aquazone Wave Racers. Younger guests will enjoy the Technicycle and the Duplo Tot Spot. There are two dining options in Technic. The Robot Pit Stop features hot dogs, nachos and ice cream. The Lakeside Sandwich Co. has a much wider selection and indoor seating.

The Great Lego Race is a mouse roller coaster on a steel frame. Riders are in small four person vehicles and the first drop provides energy for the twists and turns that follow as the vehicle rotates. This coaster usually provides more than its fair share of screams and giggles. Riders need to be at least 48 inches tall to solo ride. Guests who are at least 42 inches may ride with an adult. This was a bit of a wild ride before it was upgraded to a Virtual Reality ride. Now, riders experience the world in Legos as they climb, spin and fall in a Lego world orchestrated to the moves of the roller coaster. I can't decide if the Virtual Reality makes the ride more or less thrilling, but either way it is a fun coaster for those who like thrill rides.

Aquazone Wave Racers is a ride mostly designed to make it okay to get wet. Each Wave Racer holds two riders, who stand up to steer the vehicle. The Racers are rotated, so this is spin within a spin type of ride. Riders have water guns to shoot each other and there are also water guns for random passing guests to take a turn trying to soak riders. As a standing ride, guests must be at least 52 inches tall to go on their own, while those at least 40 inches tall may ride with an adult.

The Technicycle is a fun ride for little ones. Kids can ride by themselves starting at 42 inches while shorter siblings at least 36 inches can go with a parent. The trip to this ride is that it uses the rider's pedaling power to go up. Much like the rescue ride in Lego City, there is some built in exercise to this ride. It is a lovely ride, looking like a miniature model designed for a science fair somehow blown up to life size. As a very slow loading ride, the line for this can get long. Thankfully, there is a shaded waiting queue. If the line is longer than the shaded queue, move on to the next thing. That's going to be a painfully long wait for a very short ride.

The Duplo Tot Spot in Lego Technic is also shaded. Even the bigger kids may want to get in on the fun here. Duplo themed animals hang out in a padded play area with Duplo brings for kids to enjoy. There are benches for adults wanting to take a break from the constant walking of theme park visits. This is a great place to get some awesome photos of a little one having fun. The bright colors make for an interesting background without competing with childhood cuteness.

PIRATE COVE

Much like the restored Cypress Garden section of the park, the Pirate Cove recalls the best of prior parks with a distinctly Lego touch. Back when Cypress Gardens was the most popular theme park in Florida, a big part of the draw was a very impressive water ski show. Today, Pirate Cove features Lego soldiers and a Lego pirate, plus several human assistants, in a battle for control of the area. The show is named Battle for Brickbeard's Bounty. This is a combination stage show and water ski show. The stage show is corny. The water ski show is a collection of impressive looking feats that loosely associate with the stage show story.

While there are two large amphitheaters for viewing the show right on the water, typically only one is open for the show. The second is reserved for special events. However, we have found that a seat on the grassy spot between the two amphitheaters has a great view of the water ski show. The grass is more comfortable than the stadium seating as well as providing additional space for those who stop to see the show after it starts. The downside to this side is missing most of the story, which happens in the public theater.

The primary theater is the stage for the story and has the best view of the characters interacting. The first several rows of this stadium will get wet during the course of the show. It is a partially interactive show, as at least part of the audience will participate one way or another. Of course, in hot summer months, this may be welcome. The Battle for Brickbeard's Bounty plays several times a day. Characters from the show typically are available to meet with guests after the show.

Pirate Cove also serves as the host location for evening fireworks during special events at Legoland. Holidays such as the 4th of July get special treatment at Legoland, complete with fireworks show that can be viewed as Lego bricks exploding in the sky with the aid of 3D glasses. While the park tends to be busier on fireworks days, there is no separate ticket or admission fee required. The regular park ticket covers these special events.

We skipped Pirate's Cove our first several visits to the park. Once we took the time to watch the show once, we went back a couple of other times to try watching it from different places. Perhaps that experimentation is why we never really found this show to be all that engrossing. It is entertaining to watch, but watching the show once easily could have been plenty for Samantha and I. On the other hand, the ski boat stunts entertain my husband. We sat once in Cypress Gardens so he could watch that part of the show, including some backstage views of model citizens getting on and off the various boats. If you are more interested in the stunts than the show, it might be worth watching from this off beat location.

MINILAND

If Pirate Cove and Cypress Gardens are a mark of continuing respect for the past parks, the heart of the current park has to be Legoland's Miniland. This area of the park is a direct link back to the original Legoland park that opened in 1968 in Billund,

Denmark adjacent to the original Lego factory. That's right. Legos, which I always considered an All American toy, were invented by the Danes.

While the company got a slow start by producing wooden toys under the name Lego in 1934, by 1949 the first interlocking bricks became available. It took almost another decade before this building brick toy was refined into the post and stud Lego brick system we know today. It also took these new toys awhile to catch on internationally, as the first introductions in Germany did not go well.

While the outside world may not have been quick to enjoy the building fun, employees at the factory had a great time playing with the bricks. They built Lego statues and lined them up outside the factory. Tourists began coming to see these, traveling to Billund just to see the fancy toy statues. When this trickle of visitors expanded to 20,000 or more per year, the son of the company founder and then president Godtfred Christiansen realized there was an opportunity to create a Lego themed attraction for these tourists. This bright idea lead to the first Lego park. Originally, it was completely made up of different Lego statues and displays. Today, Legoland Billund is a full fledged theme park with themed lands, rides and other attractions drawing more than 50 million visitors since it first opened.

The heart of Legoland Billund and every subsequent Lego park, including the one in Florida, remains the Miniland in each park. These are made of miniature buildings and landscaping using the same 1:20 scale used for that first Legoland Billund exhibit. Each Legoland park around the world has unique displays that pay homage to some aspect of the host country. In Legoland Florida, guests walk through three miniature areas re-created for Florida, including the Daytona International Speedway, the Kennedy Space

Center and a large collection of different cities from the state simply named Florida. One of the most recent additions in the Florida display is a working Lego model of the Orlando Eye.

The other miniature lands in the Florida park are Pirate's Shores, California, New York, Las Vegas and Washington, DC. I would love to know what guided the choice of these locations to represent the United States in this park. Perhaps it comes down to something as simple as easily recognizable landmarks. Many of the miniature lands features a special addition. These range from buttons to push to race cars, to working lifts that move parts around, to free ranging floating boats, to soldiers marching in formation. Kids often have a blast finding the buttons that unexpectedly squirt water on innocent bystanders.

Lego has an interesting history with the Star Wars franchise. This was the first Intellectual Property Lego licensed back in 1999. It was the beginning of a very productive relationship, which currently encompasses multiple lines of Lego Star Wars sets, movies and shows. This relationship is reflected the Miniland in the Legoland parks. As a long time Star Wars fan, walking through Star Wars Miniland is one of the highlights of the trip.

Given Disney's acquisition of the Star Wars property and Galaxy's Edge in Hollywood Studios, you might wonder if this part of Legoland will continue. At a guess, I think it will. The licensing relationship between Lego and Star Wars seems profitable for both organizations. The Star Wars exhibits at Legoland really show off the best of this relationship. I think this part of the park will continue to expand to showcase Lego scenes of new movies as time goes on.

There are recreated scenes from the first six movies built in 1:20 scale Lego bricks, featuring Naboo,

Geonosis, Kashyyk & Mustafar, Tatooine, Hoth, Endor and Christophsis. Each of these worlds have some type of animation. For example, pushing a button in the Naboo recreation lifts a spaceship into the air. In Mustafar, a button starts sound effects and sends Lego Ben Kenobi and Lego Anakin Skywalker spinning into their lightsaber duel. There are also life size Lego models of Darth Maul, R2-D2 and Darth Vader in this area. These make great props for pictures.

All together, there are more than 2,000 Lego Star Wars models on display in Miniland in Florida. While the city models offer very little shade in the Florida sun, some of the Star Wars models are tucked away in a corner with some sunscreen provided by trees. It may be best to plan time viewing the models in Miniland either before or after the hottest part of the day in Florida.

It is easy to breeze through Miniland and think oh, that's cool. I did that our first couple of trips to the park. However, it was not until I took the time to stop and watch some of the models that I started noticing the real level of detail that has been poured into these recreations. Miniland functions well as the heart of the park. It shows the unique versatility of Legos and offers an attraction that only becomes more interesting after repeated exposure.

HEARTLAKE CITY

Before the Lego Movie Land or Ninjago, one of the first parts of the park to show the parent company's serious intention to invest in Legoland was the creation of Heartlake City. While it is a relatively small land with one ride, a show and a character meeting, the 2015 opening of Legoland Florida Heartlake City demonstrated the commitment of Merlin Entertainment to grow the park and highlighted the intellectual property it could use for this growth.

This part of the park builds off the popularity of the relatively new Lego Friends collection. Heartlake City, the fictional home of the five equally fictional Lego Friends, is adjacent to Fun Town. The Lego Friends were introduced in 2012. This series is very clearly and specifically targeted toward young girls. There are more than twenty Lego Friends sets with lots of white, pink and purple bricks featuring teenage girls as the five primary Lego friends. There is an animated cartoon series about the Lego Friends, which builds some story depth to these Lego sets. Lego Friends seem to function somewhat like Disney princesses by having character meets and stage shows in addition to the rides and theming in Heartlake City.

The five primary Lego Friends have distinct personalities. Mia is the Lego Friend who loves animals. She helps out at her aunt's veterinary clinic in Heartlake City. She is a vegetarian who works in the Heartlake City bakery and enjoys playing the drums. Olivia is the budding engineer in the group. She often saves the day on their adventures by coming up with plans. Olivia is sweet, shy and stubborn. Andrea is the performer in the group. She is into drama as a dancer and singer. Emma is a black belt in karate who enjoys photography and can be forgetful. Stephanie is the planner and organizer of the group, the one who pulls their social life together.

These personality traits play out in how the Friends theme is used in Heartlake City in Legoland Florida. The ride in the area, Mia's Riding Adventure, is a minor thrill ride. Guests climb about the equivalent of rocking horses on a large circular platform that then rotates while rocking up and down on the ride track. Guests who do not care much for thrill rides may want to step back and watch this one before deciding if they would like to go on Mia's Riding Adventure. Guests must be at least 48" tall to ride.

Some of the Friends meet in Stephanie's Newsroom. These meets are scheduled in an air conditioned space and the times vary slightly by day. Picking up a times guide on the way into the park is the best way to verify the exact time for all shows that day. This is usually a short wait, as it is not very well marked as a character meet.

All five of the Lego Friends are part of the live action stage show Friends to the Rescue. Andrea, as the primary performer, takes the central role in the show. If anyone in your party enjoys Lego Friends, this show is going to be a big hit. The girls leave the stage to come dance with their young admirers in the audience, who sit in two large taped areas on the floor. The best places to sit for the most interaction seem to be the front rows of either of these areas.

A stop at the Ice Cream Parlor may be just the thing on a hot day, while Sunshine Sweets will appeal to those looking for a treat. The Heartlake Mall has a great collection of Lego Friends sets as well as Disney Princess sets. There is also a Lego sculpture of the Friends in this store large enough for posing for pictures.

WATER PARK

During the summer months, the Flying School attraction stands guard to the entrance to what many kids may decide is the most fun area of Legoland – the water park. While relatively small with only seven attractions, any child who loves to swim is going to want to spend time in the water park. It's hard to classify the Water Park. For ticketing purposes, it is considered a separate, seasonal park. However, the only way to get into the Water Park is through Legoland. This makes it seem more like a land within one park, so it seems appropriate to give a brief overview here.

The first attraction most kids see in the Water Park is going to be the Duplo Splash Safari. This little play area is built for the younger kids with soft Duplo creatures who spit water and little slides that will tempt even the littlest ones to try going down and splashing into the very shallow water. There are chairs and lounges here that are claimed very quickly by the first guests in the water park. It is also adjacent to the largest restaurant in the water park, with decent views of the play area from the outer tables there.

The other attraction in the front of the water park is the lazy river. The Lego touch here includes Lego statues, some of which will squirt you, to watch as you wind along the river. There are also rubber Lego bricks that can fit on the base plates of each of the rafts. Catching these and building while floating makes for an uniquely fun experience.

Crossing the bridge to the rest of the water park, there is a small Imagination Station where guests can build little boats and race them down a Lego waterway. This is larger yet similar to the Lego raceway for little cars at the Lego store in Disney Springs. The Imagination Station has a canopy top and a couple of tables, making it a good place for parents to chill while kids race their boat creations.

Just a stone's throw away is the large wave pool. There is some Lego theming here, but it is what it is—a wave pool. The same is true for the water slides that are just across from the wave pool. The Joker Soaker, on the other hand, looks like a Lego design from the ground up. The bright colors and overall theming really fit the Lego water park. The Joker Soaker is a multi-story water play area, with random water dumps as part of the fun.

There are two different set of water slides towards the back of the park. The first two are very straightforward slides without twists or turns. The other set of slides feature both twists and turns. While these slides are all very mild, they may not appeal to those who do not like thrill rides. All of the slides are in the bright primary Lego colors, which makes this area fun to visit and photograph even if you might prefer not to go down the slides.

We usually spend a couple hours in the water park if we happen to visit when it is open. The only entrance and exit for guests to the water park is in the back of the park. This means bringing swimsuits and towels through the park for water park use and then taking them back out again. If the kids have outgrown strollers, designating one adult to fetch the water park bag then take it back out to the car might be the best way to manage this for relatively short visits to the water park.

On the other hand, I keep thinking that I would like to rent one of the cabanas at the water park and just make a day of it. Samantha would love that, as she loves the water park. If I were visiting in the summer and splurging, I would spend one day chilling in a cabana at the water park. These rentals come with a small fridge in the cabana, a ceiling fan, fabric walls that can close for privacy, a couple of lounge chairs and a dedicated server for food and beverages. The cabana rentals also come with a couple of Legoland towels. The last I checked, these cabanas go for around $100 per day. While we haven't made time to do this yet, I will one day soon.

RESORTS

When we talk about going back to Legoland, my daughter starts talking about the play areas, the master builder class and the treasure hunts. In other words, she is talking about the Legoland Hotel. To suggest she likes the resort would be a considerable understatement. The hotel is absolutely her favorite thing about the Legoland park. I am glad the lobby is considered a public area and am more than happy to order enjoy a meal from the lobby bar while she plays in the fantastic play area in the lobby. Our hotel stay at the Legoland Hotel is still one of the hotels Samantha talks about years later. This is also her #1 request for a repeat stay.

While kids love the decor, play areas and whimsical touches of the Legoland Hotel, parents will appreciate the location. The Legoland Hotel is located right at the entrance of the park. This makes time in the park extremely convenient and turns the whole Legoland experience from a quick day trip to a multi-day theme park adventure. As just one quick example, make sure you check out the Lego dragon who guards the hotel even if you don't happen to stay there.

After the success of the Legoland Hotel, which opened to the public in May 2015, the Legoland resort followed with a second hotel, called the Beach Retreat, less than two years later in April of 2017. The second resort is more budget friendly. It is located about a mile from the park on the lake. It features a separate drive-through check in, pool, play areas, restaurant and consists of different bungalows themed to a Lego beach adventure. This location offers perhaps more privacy but fewer perks. The rooms also seem smaller to me.

The second hotel is called the Beach Retreat and it is a quick five minute drive away. The Beach Retreat is a budget friendlier option that includes several of the elements that make the Legoland Hotel so much fun. The Beach Retreat is much more spread out and features single story bungalows around central areas with play equipment or other community areas. Each bungalow holds two hotel rooms. Each room has one king bed, a bathroom and a small alcove with two bunk beds and the pull out trundle. These rooms do not feature the treasure hunt and are smaller than the rooms in the Legoland hotel. These differences, along with a location further from the park, result in the Beach Retreat being a lower cost alternative to the Legoland Hotel. While neither hotel offers the range of dining or activities that a moderate or deluxe Disney property will offer, both are excellent choices for enhancing a Legoland visit.

TAKING IT ALL IN

Legoland is the park built for kids. This place is designed and built for families. We enjoy our visits there and have happily brought friends and family along to enjoy it as well. While the park is growing and adding new experiences, it remains an easy park to visit. Minimal planning is needed to have an awesome time. Now that we have an overview of what is in the park, let's turn to different ways to enjoy a vacation at Legoland.

CHAPTER TWO

Day Tripping Legoland from Disney World

One way to enjoy time at Legoland is to add a day to a trip to Disney World. This is a popular option. It is so popular, in fact, that I can entertain myself at Legoland by counting the number of Legoland guests who show up wearing Disney tee shirts and trying to guess how many have come to visit Legoland as one day of their Disney World vacation.

Walt Disney World operates on a far larger scale than Legoland. A quick google search will show even the most casual planner there is more to do at Walt Disney World than can be done on a single vacation. By comparison, the same kind of quick search will suggest Legoland is a one day park, with plenty to do but all of it doable in one day with some minimal planning.

One specific example of this difference is shown in park hours. While even in slow season, Disney is typically a 9am to 9pm park, Legoland may only be open 10am to 5pm. The easy math there suggests a Disney park is about almost twice as long as the Legoland park on any given day. More importantly for those considering day tripping from Disney to Legoland, that one hour later opening means those who drive down from Disney are still getting up about the same time to get to Legoland at 10am as getting to Magic Kingdom at

9am due to the drive. We thought that was reasonable as my husband, like most sensible people, prefers to stay in one hotel on vacation rather than jumping from hotel to hotel. Adding a day to a Disney trip to visit Legoland seemed reasonable. And that's exactly what we did on our first visit to Legoland.

So we woke up bright and early on the first full day of our vacation and set out for Legoland. The first clue we didn't do as much research as usual was missing the exit. That worked out okay, as we took the next exit and had a much more adventurous drive. Going this way meant we saw some of the older part of the area. I got such a kick out of seeing the old fashioned fast food signs. It was like taking a step back a couple of decades to being a kid myself, which was a great frame of mind for enjoying a park built for kids.

Arriving at the park, we paid the parking fee and made our way to the ticket booth. At the time, an annual pass was only slightly more than a single day ticket. Still not sure we'd ever want to do more than one day, we waited and waited and waited and waited in the ticket booth line. Seriously, this took far more time than I expected. Once we had our tickets, walking over and into the park was easy.

We accidentally visited Legoland during one of the best times of the year—the Christmas season. By the time we walked by the giant Lego Christmas tree and met a couple of characters, it was obvious we would come back. So after a couple of rides, we found guest services in the park and upgraded to annual passes. Aside from my minor personal irritation that we would not get reimbursed for the parking fee when we upgraded to the annual pass, stopping in to guest services was a lot of fun! The Model Citizen who helped us played with my daughter, who was fascinated that everything on the counter was made from or encased in Legos. The welcome pack included a couple of special Lego pieces and the usual pamphlets and information. I think we were in and out in maybe 20 minutes.

Once we decided to get annual passes, we relaxed. We slowed down, knowing we would be back to enjoy the park over several trips. It has taken a few years for me to learn this works better for our family. We just are not the type that does well with the commando touring strategy. We like to enjoy the small things. Our daughter will happily spend an hour or more in a play area. With annual passes, it is easy to stop and spend this time. Back when we did family trips with day tickets, I always wanted to push past the parts of the trip that my husband and daughter enjoy most. It is not coincidence that our trips became more fun when I relaxed and learned to go with the flow, at least to some extent, on our vacations.

Samantha saw the Lego Friends area next so we followed her to check it out. The Heartlake City Friends are the closest Lego equivalent we have seen to the Disney princesses. My daughter loves these characters. The five primary Lego Friends are Stephanie, the confident leader who enjoys sports and stories; Olivia, the smart environmentalist who is both kind and clumsy; Emma, the fashionable girl who loves to ride horses; Mia, the vegetarian who loves animals; and Andrea, the musically gifted performer in the group. These friends work together to help solve problems in Heartlake city. Overall, these girls are portrayed with part time jobs, studying for school and in general being quite decent role models for kids. My little girl adores these characters and enjoys interacting with them at Legoland.

In Legoland, Heartlake City has basically three attractions. There is a ride, a character meet and a character show. While she wasn't willing to do the ride because it looked scary, she really enjoyed the live show featuring the Friends. All five of the Friends are part of this show. There is singing, dancing, a simple plot and some confetti falling from the ceiling at the end of the show. If your child is interested in interacting with the characters like mine, try for a front row spot on the floor in one of the two taped off sections. That's the best spot to get a high five, hand shake or even being pulled out to dance with one or more of the characters when they work the floor. If you happen to visit during the summer, this would be a good afternoon break in an air conditioned building. Just be aware it is like the Disney Junior show in Hollywood Studios—all seating is on the floor. If adults prefer to stand, they will be asked to stand in the back of the room so other guests can see.

Adjacent to the Friends area is the pizza buffet. We were surprised by how much we liked the pizza here, with salad, bread and some other pasta as a nice bonus. The annual pass yielded its first savings here with 10% off the meal. This restaurant is entirely self serve, with soda and tea dispensers for drinks and the buffet offerings.

The Lego mini-land is fascinating. There are recreations of different buildings and whole city scapes. There is a space shuttle launch pad and the Daytona race track. Las Vegas is there in all its glory as is Washington, DC. Many of these outdoor displays have buttons for the kids to press, some of which shoot water on unsuspecting parents. Not all buttons trigger a shower. Some just start some action in the display. Rockets may launch, pirates may attack, soldiers may march or music may start to play. I could easily spend hours playing with these miniature lands.

Just off this main mini-land there is a separate Star Wars mini land. My husband saw his dream toy there—a recreated Millennium Falcon roughly the size of the giant early satellite dishes from the 1980s. If we ever win the lottery, I know what to get him. There are also scenes from the different movies, ranging from Tatooine to Hoth to Jakku. Taking a little while to walk through some favorite movie memories was fun here.

Then we needed to decide if we would watch the afternoon pirate show, explore Cypress Gardens, which is both the oldest part of the park and a botanical garden or go do more rides. Know we would be back, we decided to come back in the spring when the garden would be in bloom and try for both a few more rides and the show. We made it to the back of the park, then spent the rest of the afternoon playing on the rides there.

Day tripping Legoland while staying at Disney World for a mostly Disney vacation, we did not see the pirate show, any of the movies at the theater or explore the gardens and only did half the rides on one slow day at the park. Certainly we could have done at least a couple of these by moving more quickly. Still, I'm not sure that anyone could do everything at the park in the seven hours it is open on slow days. That is one of the downsides of planning a day at Legoland while staying at Disney. You can do a great deal but you won't see everything. The other downside was the drive back to Disney. It is only 45 minutes but with a tired child it felt much longer.

Since one of the primary reasons for writing this book is to help others learn from our mistakes, I am just going to flat out say it—- driving down for a day trip from Disney World is not the ideal way to experience Legoland. As soon as we pulled in and saw the Legoland hotel, it was obvious that's where we should have stayed for a trip to Legoland. Why? It goes back to "location, location, location." Yes, you can fit many attractions at Legoland in a day. However, it would not be fun to push a young child to get it all in one day. Kids in a theme park need breaks. And so do parents, for that matter. The Legoland hotel is perhaps a couple hundred feet from the park entrance. The ability to go back to the room and chill for awhile would have been absolutely marvelous. We did not have that on our first visit and we missed it.

Also, the drive from Disney World to Legoland is not all that entertaining. It's not bad, just a long drive in the country. Anyone driving with kids is going to want to have some options in the car to entertain the kids. I have found that a small container of Legos is a good way to give our daughter something to play with and set her up for a fun time in the park. We have also used the Color Wonder markers and coloring books. Those are great because the ink only works on the special paper, avoiding the possibility of art decorating the car. There are almost always books in the back seat for her. We had a couple of the early reader books with Lego themes. I understand there are Lego themed books for kids of all ages. Much like having the Legos themselves in the car, this really fits the theme for driving to Legoland! And, well, yes, sometimes we go to the electronic babysitter and let her play with her kindle or watch a show on a tablet. Headphones for kids in cars are a good thing.

I should also add that we had an additional motivation for getting annual passes at Legoland, which was to come back and visit the water park when it was open. This is included in the annual pass cost. However, the park is only open during the warmer months. Knowing that we would want to come back and visit at least the water park section of the park, the annual pass was realistically the best option for us. If your family happens to visit during the spring or summer, you may be able to get everything in on a one day trip. It is important to understand on the front end that doing everything in one day means the family will be moving the whole day. That can be a lot to add to an already busy Disney World vacation.

Reading back over that last paragraph, I sound like a used car salesperson. Really, I am not out for commission or anything—just sharing that the Annual Pass wound up being the best option for my family. So while I may have overshared our ticket logic, choosing which ticket to get for Legoland is fairly simple. If you plan to day trip from Disney, get the best discount you can find on the single day tickets. If you think two days sound like a better pace, a little searching will likely find a two day ticket for minimal additional cost over the one day ticket. With this option, remember that you will pay for parking both days. This may well add more than the incremental cost of a two day ticket over a one day ticket than the additional park day. However, if you think that you might do more than two days, or if you want to come back at some point in the next 365 days or are considering a Legoland hotel stay, it is worth evaluating an annual pass.

Let's talk about that hotel discount for the annual pass for a moment. I had an eye on a Legoland visit for a long time before we actually made the trip. I had priced a night at the Legoland hotel during this trip to Orlando but decided against it because of the cost. Yes, that's right; staying at one of the value resorts at Disney World was less expensive than staying at the Legoland hotel when I priced both options online. But once we were actually at Legoland visiting, both Craig and I could see the value of staying right there, far closer to the park than any of the Disney deluxe resorts are to any of the Disney parks.

So after upgrading to annual passes, I fed my husband pizza and negotiated a return to Legoland for the following weekend if I could get a decent rate for the Legoland hotel. We stopped by the hotel on the way back to the car. Happily, the Friday night we wanted was a very slow night at the hotel. Using the annual passholder discount and quite possibly some other front desk magic, I was given a great price. Literally, it was less than 50% of the best price I had previously seen on the website for that night. I immediately booked it and we had our second visit to Legoland planned before we left the first one.

CHAPTER THREE

The Hotel is Awesome

Our first day trip to Legoland from Disney World was enough to interest us in returning quickly. In fact, we booked our second trip before leaving the property. So after our first few hours in Legoland, we then spent five days at Disney World before returning to Legoland. I guess you could call it a Lego sandwich trip!

One of the reasons I write these books is to share what we tend to have to learn the hard way so that others can make better decisions. One of the things we learned from Disney World was that staying close to the parks made the whole trip easier and a ton more fun. I hoped the same would be the case at Legoland. Actually, it was even more significant than I expected. If you only want to visit Legoland once, staying at the hotel onsite will make the trip much more convenient and much more fun. Just be prepared to pay for the benefit, as staying onsite at the Legoland hotel is significantly more expensive than other nearby options.

After packing up and playing in Disney World on a Friday morning, we arrived at Legoland around 2pm, which is a little ahead of the 4pm check in time. We parked and walked to the hotel to see if the room was ready. A cheesy fun sign asking "Argggggggg ya ready to have some fun?" with a Lego pirate caught my eye. Yep, I thought to myself, that's Legoland. Here's hoping that translates to fun in the hotel and in the park.

As the hotel is basically in the parking lot, there is no way to miss it. Our little girl was more than ready to check out the hotel. Opening the door into the lobby makes it clear this is a hotel for kids & kids-at-heart who love Legos. As you walk into the lobby, there is a Lego bellman and a Lego bed. Let the fun begin, Lego style.

The wall behind the check in counter is covered in mini Lego figures. A large Lego boy rides a bicycle while carrying a surfboard in front of the mini figures. Seasonal Lego art decorates the counter top. Just past the check in counter, there is a large pit of Legos. Two support beams are in the middle of this Lego pit. They are partially covered by stacks of Lego boards wrapping the beams from the floor and the ceiling. This pit of Legos is available 24/7 for hotel guests or anyone who happens to want to play in the lobby. Samantha and Craig spent a lot of time here building with the Legos.

The lobby also plays home to a fantastic themed kids play area. With clever use of space, this includes a floor to ceiling Lego castle, complete with ogres and knights, plus a Lego pirate ship with mermaid figurehead, plus a play space with a large Lego tree and blackboard for drawing. And there are a few other Lego touches around the lobby. In December for example, these touches include Lego Christmas trees complete with Lego decorations on the trees.

One of the lobby elements that struck me as very thoughtful towards a target clientele of families with small children, the lobby also includes what is essentially a quiet room. Just off the bar area, a hallway leads to the Master Builder class and restrooms. Off that hallway, there is a smaller room a little away from the main action in the lobby with chairs, tables and yes, more Lego bricks for guests to enjoy at their leisure. The main play area can get noisy in the evenings and this side room might be a better choice for younger or shyer children.

The adults are not forgotten. Immediately adjacent to the play area is the Skyline Lounge. Comfortable chairs in very bright colors compliment the high energy feel of the area while giving adult a place to sit and keep an eye on their kids while indulging in a drink. The menu, while basic, has a decent variety of options for both food and drink.

The Legoland Hotel is a wonderfully themed and very small hotel. It has only around 150 total rooms. Even if you stuff all those rooms to max capacity, that's still only around 750 total hotel guests at any given time. Based on the large number of available rooms & easy complimentary upgrade, my guess is the hotel was virtually empty the night we were there. It may not be possible to convey just how much fun we had as a family in our single night at the Legoland Hotel. In many ways, it was like the best parts of the theme park experience continued in a smaller, more comfortable venue.

Starting at check in, there is a sense this is a different type of hotel. This came through clearly to me when the Model Citizen at the check in desk asked me which Master Builder session would my child preferred to attend. I must have had a hesitant look, as she rapidly clarified these were complimentary sessions for hotel guests. Curious, I asked how many she could sign up to attend. The answer was—as many as she wants, as long as there are open spaces in the class.

I was not sure what to expect from this Master Builder class. You take your child to the classroom tucked in the back of the first floor of the hotel. There are chairs along the walls where parents are welcome to stay and watch the class. Or parents can choose to step out to the lounge that is only a few steps away from the class. I opted to stay with my daughter for this class. After all, I am a Lego fan too. The idea that she would get free Legos as well as personal instruction from a Lego Master Builder on how to put together the exclusive set of free Legos was not something I was going to skip.

It was a lot of fun to watch the Master Builder class. The teacher, who is a Lego Master Builder, had sets of Legos at each student table with all the parts for the build. She built the model on the front desk, which was projected up on a large screen so that all the kids could easily follow along. She did a great job of watching the children, some of whom were quite skilled while others could barely snap the bricks together and keeping them on task. She also entertained her group with stories about Legoland, different builds and some of the Lego builds on display in the Master Builder classroom. This helped the time fly by quickly and almost before we knew it, all the kids had finished their build. All of the classes for the weekend we were at the Legoland Hotel were for the same build set, a Lego Kangaroo. That explained in part why guests were welcome to sign up for multiple classes. Relatively few were going to be interested in building the same thing again and again and again.

There were a few other clues that this hotel was going to be a different experience for us at check in as well. First, there were Lego poinsettias and gift boxes on the counter. Next, there was a wall of Lego minifigures lining the wall behind the desk. Third, everywhere you looked, the brightly decorated lobby held the laughter of kids at play or the distraction of some fun Lego element. Once we were checked in, the Model Citizen smiled at me and said she hoped we enjoyed the elevator.

My first thought on hearing this was actually of the Tower of Terror. I had a flash of some kind of strange Lego themed Twilight zone, where we would be bounced up, down and all around before being spit out into a Lego hallway. Fortunately, while the elevator is creative and fun, it is not that adventurous. Instead, the two hotel elevators feature a disco ball, disco themed wall panels and a floor made of some type of gel that changes under your feet when dances. And of course there is disco music to compliment the decor. Samantha was dancing before we got to the second floor. We ran into other families several times who were simply riding the elevators up and down at their children's request so they could keep dancing and playing in them.

Although Samantha would have happily continued dancing her way up and down the elevator with her new friends, we insisted on getting out on our floor to go check out the room. Samantha was delighted to find that we were on the Friends themed hallway. There are actually several different possible themed rooms in the Legoland Hotel. There are pirate rooms. There are adventure rooms. There are kingdom rooms. There are Friends rooms. And coming in 2019, there will be rooms themed to the Lego Movie 2. Each of these themed rooms are highly decorated, with a lot of thought put into the small details that make the room seem playful.

What type of details? Well, let's start with the Lego cat. That was the first thing our daughter noticed. Then she caught sight of the kids area. We lost her for a moment of amazement when she realized she had bunk beds and her own TV for the evening. There were cute cards in the room, specifying the room was inspected and found to be monster free. We had fun with that one, as both the Mommy Monster and the Daddy Monster invaded Samantha's space to help her with the treasure hunt.

Well of course there is a treasure hunt. What kind of hotel room doesn't come with a treasure hunt? This may well have been our favorite part of the Legoland hotel experience, because it was so unexpected. There is a note with a series of puzzles to solve, which then gives the code to unlock the treasure box in the room. All of the loot in the treasure box—Lego sets, juice pouches and the like—are gifts to the children who figure out the code to the box.

As the treasure hunt shows, designers put a good deal of thought into creating a hotel room that would entertain children. That small level of thoughtfulness shows in other details, such as a toilet insert that makes it easier for toddlers to use the toilet and a small step for children to use to more easily reach the sink. Along these same lines, there is a detachable shower head which is very useful for cleaning a small child and touches like nightstands on both sides of the king size bed so that both parents can have a place to put their stuff and charge their phones.

The one place this drive for usefulness goes too far for my personal taste is the lack of doors on the closet. I can see that open storage areas make it easier to find stuff but I prefer being able to close off my closet mess. However, the Keurig in the room and a nice assortment of pods, including one hot chocolate option, was nice. The room also had a welcome packet, with information on the park show times, a map and a list of hotel activities.

It took us a bit to realize there were beds for three children, not just two. Samantha loves bunk beds when she can have the top bunk. The room included the two bunk beds plus a trundle bed that pulls out from underneath the bottom bunk beds. Three kids could sleep in the space very comfortably. I tried out the bottom bunk bed. It is comfortable and tall enough for me. My husband would not fit easily on this bed, as he is too tall. On the other hand, the king size bed for adults was very comfortable.

The hotel theming is not limited to the room, lobby and elevator. The different themed rooms are on themed floors that match the rooms. While the themed floors have different types of rooms, most of the rooms are standard rooms. We were in a standard room. Those have the adult area with a king sized bed, dresser and chair. The bathroom is between the adult area and the space designed for children with bunk beds. Storage, including closet space, is across from the bathroom. The standard rooms sleep five and are designed for two adults in the king bed, one child in the upper bunk bed, one child in the bottom bunk bed and one child in the trundle that pulls out underneath the bottom bunk bed. This area also includes a separate TV for the kids and sufficient floor space to play. Premium rooms have the same footprint with additional theming and toys in the room for kids to enjoy. There are also a limited number of accessible rooms available in each theme.

Overall, the Legoland hotel floor plan feels much larger than the 360 square feet reported for the rooms. Space has been maximized for family enjoyment. That does mean that some of the things I've come to expect from hotels such as ergonomic desks, USB hubs and comfortable chairs are not part of the rooms. Instead, the floorplan is designed to give adults and children separate spaces. As a mom, I heartily approve of this plan for family travel.

At some point in the future, we may be able to indulge in one of the VIP suites. These are a little more than double the square footage of the standard rooms at around 800 square feet. The VIP suites allow for up to 9 guests by adding a living space with a sleeper

sofa and a second set of bunk beds to the room. There
is also more space in the bathroom and a generous
screened balcony off the suite in addition to a play area
for the kids separate from their bedroom space.

At the Legoland Hotel, characters come out and
play with kids in the Legoland hotel lobby. This is a
fantastic compliment to the already fun themed play
areas. These play dates are not the only opportunity
for hotel guests to interact with characters. Breakfast
in the hotel restaurant is included with the room price.
Not only is the food excellent, it is a complementary
character breakfast. I'll stop a second to let long time
Disney fans stop and contemplate that last sentence.
Complimentary. Character. Meal.

The morning we had breakfast at the hotel, three
of the Lego Friends characters joined us. The rotation
of Lego characters meeting guests in the lobby and
play area is much broader. There are some characters
in full body and face suits that replicate popular
Lego characters like Emmet and Wyldstyle from the
Lego Movie. There are others in costume as pirate
queens or adventurer knights or chivalrous princes.
After breakfast, the Friends characters also moved
to the lobby. Andrea, one of the Lego Heartlake
City Friends characters, spent over an hour playing
with Samantha in the hotel lobby this morning.
Checking in early gave us time to drop our stuff off,
check out the lobby, play in the room and still walk
into the park for an hour. Just a week after our last
visit, I noticed that the giant Lego Christmas tree
had more decorations on it. We enjoyed another ride
on the Island in the Sky and Samantha took a ride on
her favorite carousel horse. Then we found our way to
the castle to play. This was a lot of fun as my daughter
had visited the princess makeover at Bibbity Bobbity
Boutique at Disney the day before and still had her

hair up in the fancy hairdo with her princess dress on. She liked finding another castle and giggled while asking for fresh face paint in the castle courtyard.

While we did not indulge our princess in face paint, we did take her to a ride we missed on the first visit, the Royal Joust Ride. Well, perhaps that is not quite the right way to say that. This particular ride is only for small kids, no parents allowed. Kids climb on board Lego styled horses that look like large rocking horses to me. The horses follow a track, where parents can watch the entire ride and easily capture photos or videos.

Right across from the horse ride is a large play area named the Forestmen's Hideout. This is a fun play area and would be a great place for kids with more energy than their parents to play after lunch. We did a quick walk through and promised she could play here more later. Craig and I wanted to go back for another look at the Star Wars portion of mini-land before the park closed. We are Star Wars fans and really enjoyed these displays.

As the park began to close, we started walking back to our room. Seeing one fun surprise, we stopped for a photo with a Lego Santa, Lego sleigh and Lego reindeer. All of the Orlando area theme parks decorate for Christmas and it was nice to see Legoland participating in this tradition.

Back in the hotel lobby, we saw several Lego characters had come out to play. We opted to stay and play as well. That is, Samantha played while we ordered dinner at the bar and hung out to watch her play with the other children and characters in the play area. There were some organized activities, such as a build competition and other games, but mostly the kids ran around the play area castle and made up their own games. I pulled Samantha away from the fun in time to go participate in the Master Builder class. When we came back to the main play area, we found she had won the build competition in her age bracket. She proudly took home a nice certificate and enjoyed a specialty kids drink in the bar.

After the nightly lobby entertainment ends, which was around 8pm that night, there is not much to do. That works well with the overall theme and intended audience of Legoland. This park is built to appeal to younger kids. At some point, maybe around age 10, I expect my daughter to age out and lose interest in this park. Until then, one of the reasons we enjoy Legoland is that the hours work for young kids on a typical early to bed school driven schedule. In fact, hotel quiet hours start at 10, easily allowing us to stay on a more typical sleep schedule. This is a big win on vacation, as a well rested family has more fun that a tired family.

After a full night's sleep, there was a surprise waiting for us outside the door when we headed downstairs for breakfast. Legoland publishes a newspaper for hotel guests. It is cute, with tongue in cheek humor. However, the most entertaining part might have been watching my daughter, who is totally a child of the digital age, try to figure out what to do with this folded up big piece of a paper. Laughing, I tucked it under my arm and we took the disco elevator down to breakfast with a promise I would help her open it and read it at the table.

Breakfast is included in the hotel cost for guests. Legoland has joined the irritating current trend for hotels to charge guests a resort fee on top of the nightly rate. I do not like this trend as it makes it harder to compare cost apples-to-apples and seems more like a greed fee than a legitimate expense. If resorts have somehow managed to provide internet, work out rooms and perhaps small bottles of water as part of the nightly rate for years (decades), why do these items suddenly require a seperate charge?

However, because of all the extras at the Legoland hotel, I can almost accept the fee here as legitimate. Between the nightly lobby entertainment, the complimentary breakfast, the Master Builder class, the in-room treasure hunt and the little touches like the newspaper, I can actually see the resort fee covering these items. I still think it would be better to include this in the nightly rate rather than as a separate line item, but at least here I can understand it.

Walking in the buffet area, the first thing to catch my eye was the beverage station. As much of the station as possible is covered in Legos. That theme continues with the center buffer, which features Lego holders for plates and utensils. The labels for the food sit in Lego photo frames. The chef wore a very creative homemade Lego hat. Plus there are Lego decorations everywhere and the restaurant area is in the bright primary colors of Lego blocks.

The other thing I noticed was the lowered height of the central buffet with the most kid friendly food. This makes is easier for kids to make their own plates and is another example of the thought and detail that went into make the hotel so family friendly for small kids.

As far as food, all the typical breakfast buffet items are available. There are eggs, waffles, pancakes, grits, omelette, bacon, sausage, cereals, yogurts, fruit and many bread options. The buffet also features some less typical options, such as salmon and slushies. Several items were individually packaged, so if a family slept in or was otherwise running late, rushing through to grab some items to go would be an option.

I am glad we had plenty of time for breakfast in the restaurant. Getting breakfast to go would eliminate the morning entertainment. Characters join guests for meals. Perhaps due to the fact that the hotel was extremely slow when we were there, the characters were not in any hurry at all. One of the Friends sat with Samantha and showed her how to open that newspaper I mentioned. They read together for a good ten minutes, with the character adding comments that made my daughter giggle. Both girls—character and guest— were obviously having a good time playing together. It was almost a shame to gently urge the character to move on to the next family so my daughter would eat.

We enjoyed the breakfast buffet. We did not do the evening buffet, partially due to the cost of the buffet but mostly because of the convenience of eating bar food adjacent to the play area. Some of the families we chatted with also mentioned the bar food was better than the dinner buffet. I don't have an opinion on that, but in general while I like breakfast buffets our luck has been more hit or miss on dinner buffets.

After breakfast, we saw Adventurer LegoMan meeting in the lobby. Samantha absolutely refused to go near him. She does not have an appreciation for non human characters at the moment. On the other hand, when the Lego Friend Andrea came over to play Legos with Samantha, she was more than happy to play. I realized that there was no way we were going to walk over in time to enjoy the early park time that is a perk for hotel guests. Craig offered to stay with her and catch up to me when Samantha & Andrea were done playing.

Knowing our child was safe and happy with her father, I took the fifty or so steps out of the hotel and through the gates to Legoland. Although I still maintain the park is designed and built for a target audience of the under ten set, I will admit that I enjoyed the time to meander around by myself. I enjoy taking pictures and there are lots of good photos to be taken in the park. While I played, my husband and daughter packed up and checked us out of the hotel.

After loading the car, Craig and Samantha joined me in the park. They were ready to ride the rides and see a show at the theater. That 4D show in the theater was fun, right up to the point the mist hit and Samantha decided that wasn't funny at all. Her father and I didn't help much, as we were busy laughing at each other for being startled.

On the way back out we stopped in the Big Store to pick up a souvenir. I thought that would be a quick ten minute in and out. There were far too many choices for that. Eventually, we each picked out a Lego set as a memory of the trip and to give us something to do before our next visit. Samantha cheerfully chatted about visiting Legoland on the way out of the park, waving goodbye to the Lego statues and promising to come visit again soon.

CHAPTER FOUR

Stretching a Dollar Staying Off Property

Samantha kept her promise to come visit Legoland again soon. Not quite two months later, we had a big trip to Disney World planned with friends. Since we had the time, I wanted to find a way to spend a day or two at Legoland before our friends arrived for the Disney trip. However, given the budget busting Disney trip already planned, I needed to find a way to do this Legoland weekend as inexpensively as possible. So while I really wanted to stay at the Legoland hotel again, instead we booked a couple of nights at the Hampton Inn in Winter Haven. We had plenty of hotel points to cover the nights we wanted to stay. That's good, because between the annual passes from the prior trip and free hotel nights, adding on this weekend to a planned Disney trip cost almost nothing.

This hotel is one of the Legoland partner hotels. It is a nice, comfortable little hotel. While most Hamptons are remarkably consistent, occasionally you find a dated one that is not in good shape. That's not the case here. This Hampton is in good shape and I would book another stay here without hesitation. Not only is the Hampton comfortable and convenient, I can always find ways to use money saved to plan another trip. I particularly liked the Lego bellman figure right by the main door at the Hampton. This cheerful fellow is the first thing you see upon walking in and the last sight when walking out. He makes an excellent ambassador for the hotel.

At the time, Legoland benefits for staying at this Hampton included Lego figures in the lobby, a shuttle to and from the park and some fun complimentary postcards with Lego themes for kids to color and send home. My favorite hotel touch this trip was the welcome pack. There was the normal Hampton bag with bottles of water. Also in that little bag were several pieces of individually wrapped Lego shaped chocolate candy. Chocolate candy Lego bricks are now officially my favorite welcome gift.

There are several other chain hotels in the area that make good, budget friendly alternatives to the Legoland Hotel. In fact, this Hampton shares a parking lot with a Holiday Inn. This gives easy meal options, as a Red Lobster and Outback are essentially in the same parking lot. If fast food is a better fit, there are also a Chick-fil-a, Boston Market and Panera on the same block and these are easy walking options. For those who might prefer Starbucks to hotel coffee, that is also an easy walk of a block or less.

After checking into the hotel and picking up the chocolate brick welcome gift, we unpacked and settled in the room quickly. It was a fairly standard hotel room – bed, bathroom, desk and a couple of chairs. There are the usual options of either two beds or a single king bed. At the time, we traveled so frequently I wanted to find a way to bring a bit of home along for my daughter. We did that with an inflatable toddler bed from Walmart that fits easily in a small suitcase or even a child's backpack.

The inflatable bed features a mattress that fits inside a surround of inflatable walls. While the bed is marketed for toddlers, it fit Samantha until she was more than four feet tall. This inflatable bed fit easily in the center of a double bed if we booked a room with two beds or on the floor in less space than a twin bed if we opted for a room with a single king bed. We also used this inflatable toddler bed many nights in hotels that had a king bed plus a convertible sofa bed. The security of having short little walls surrounding the mattress on all sides gave my daughter a comforting sense of security.

In fact, there were several nights at home she asked for her hotel bed. Samantha loved the consistency of having her own her favorite sheets, blanks and stuffed animals to make up her hotel bed. One of the things we learned with traveling so frequently with a young child was to find ways to give her some control of her environment. This travel bed and later options like an indoor tent allowed us to keep her with us while also giving her some space of her own.

Getting to the hotel late meant Samantha was asleep almost as soon as we got her ready for bed. She may fight waking up during a normal school day, but on vacation the child is usually up and ready to go by 6am. That is a very good thing when visiting theme parks, as the early guests typically enjoy lower crowds in the parks. I keep telling myself that when she wakes me at 5am when we are on vacation, anyway!

The next morning, Legoland opened at 10am. However, Legoland hotel guests and annual pass holders are invited to enjoy an early opening time of 9:30am. Samantha's early wake up schedule gave us plenty of time to enjoy a leisurely complimentary breakfast at the Hampton before heading out. This is a fairly basic breakfast. There are hot and cold cereal options, a couple of basic hot breakfast items that rotate daily, some coffee selections, yogurt and fruit plus a waffle bar. Happily, this gives us all the ingredients needed to make a strawberry and whipped cream waffles, which are a family favorite.

The customer service at the Hampton was great. One of the people I very much enjoyed was the lady who looked after the breakfast. She came by and visited with everyone to make sure they enjoyed the meal. She also brought coloring pages and crayons for tables with kids. The truly thoughtful touch was the couple of postcards she brought for my daughter to color and mail home. As a courtesy to guests, these kid friendly, Hampton Winter Haven themed postcards can be dropped off with the hotel front desk for courtesy postage and delivery via the US mail. Samantha took her time to make a postcard special for her grandmother. Then we walked it over to the front desk, where another kind Hampton employee stamped it for us and promised to get it out with Monday morning's mail.

We left the Hampton well fed and ready for the day's adventures early. The hotel is only 10 minutes from the park, so we drove ourselves over with a stop at a local store along the way. We could have easily waited for the complimentary transportation from the hotel to the park. There are multiple scheduled times per day for guests to catch a ride over in the morning and back to the hotel in the afternoons. Maybe one day we will do this but I doubt it. We prefer the freedom to come and go at whim while traveling.

In fact, on the way to the park that morning, we decided on a whim to stop and shop for some mini figures to trade with Legoland Model Citizens. Much like Disney Cast Members do pin trading, Legoland Model Citizens will trade mini-figures. I was disappointed with the available Lego selections at the store. Reasonably enough, if you want to buy Legos in Winter Haven, the best bet is to go to Legoland. So even after stopping to check other options, we went with the make your own minifigure pack in Legoland. These are around $10 for a set of three minifigures. Plus Samantha enjoys making these, so getting these in the park worked out fine.

I should add that I did eventually find a way to buy some mini-figures to use to trade in the park. Amazon offers several different mini-figure sets, many quite reasonably priced. We went with one of the sellers who offered free Prime delivery and had excellent customer feedback. Sure enough, a couple of days after ordering, we had a set of twenty brand new Lego mini-figures to put together and play with. The only downside to this is that Samantha has yet to be willing to part with any of these new treasures in order to do the trading.

Getting to Legoland, we parked and grabbed our backpacks. Our typical backpack items include water bottles, camera, blankets, sunscreen, snacks and some type of toy like bubbles to entertain Samantha while waiting in line. I have tried skipping these heavy backpacks a couple of times. Both times, that was a mistake. It is worth carrying the backpacks to have what we need available when we want it.

One thing we forgot this trip was the security screening. After some incidents early in 2016, all the Orlando theme parks began doing additional screening prior to allowing guests into ticket areas or parks. My husband typically carries a pocket knife. He has forgotten to take it out and leave it in the car a couple of times. At least it is a short walk back to the car at Legoland, as when he forgot about the pocket knife at Magic Kingdom we wound up renting a locker for it for the day rather than going all the way back to the Ticket and Transportation Center. Craig insisted we go on into the park while he returned to the car. That was fine, as it is easy to meet back up in Legoland.

Once in the park, our daughter knew exactly where she wanted to do. She tugged my hand and took us to the Farm play area in Duplo Valley. This is the building that looks like a barn and houses the indoor play area as well as the baby center. With barely a backward glance to make sure I was still there, she took off to meet new friends and play. It is great to be able to give Samantha an hour or so to play in a really neat themed play area if that is what she wants to do on vacation. At the risk of repeating myself, this is one of the advantages of an annual pass for our family. I would not be able to relax and enjoy these slow moments while trying to maximize every moment on a day pass.

After play time in the barn, Samantha wanted to spend the rest of the morning on the rides in Duplo Valley. These two simple, straightforward rides are fun as she can see the entire ride and predict what is going to happen. At this age, she doesn't like surprises on rides. Craig and I switched taking her on the Tractor ride. But given the small size of the Train, Samantha was on her own for that one. That is one watch out for parents at Legoland. Some of the rides are designed for child-sized humans, not adult sized. Encouraging our child to ride independently on some of these rides has been a good plan for us.

That afternoon, we caught the pirate show for the first time. This is worth the time to watch. It is built off the water skiing history on this lake. It is about a 20 minute show and features a brave heroine protecting treasure from Lego pirates. There is the possibility of splash in the first few rows, so this might be one where sitting up higher and a little further away from the action is a good thing unless you want to get wet on a hot day. After the pirate show, we revisited the Friends show then called it good and headed back to the hotel for a quick dinner and early night.

The next morning, after checking out of the Hampton, I dropped Craig and Samantha off at Legoland while I went to take care of a few errands. When I came back to rejoin them, I was surprised to learn they never made it into the park. Instead, Samantha wanted to go play in the play area in the hotel lobby. Craig was happy to hang with her there. She really likes that hotel.

As I got back around lunch time, we ate at the bar to give Samantha some more play time. Then we walked into the park for while. We found the pressed penny machines and had fun making a few for her collection. Then we visited a few rides to watch her captain a Lego boat and drive a Lego car, play some more and try to talk us into playing one of the carnival games. Seeing one with a guaranteed win, we let her play one game. She won a stuffed animal and was delighted about it. Thinking that was a good way to leave the park on a high note, we left Legoland to go meet our friends at the Animal Kingdom and start the Disney portion of the trip.

I strongly considered doing the Lego hotel for the two nights at the beginning of this trip. I really wanted to stay there again, both because it was so easy and because Samantha loves the hotel. But I just could not justify the cost given the planned expenses for the rest of the trip. I think we wound up with the best of both worlds with the time in the hotel lobby and free nights at the Hampton Inn using points.

Still, if time to plan and vacation budget allow, families considering a visit to Legoland are best served by a night or two at the Legoland Hotel. Even trips planned primarily for Disney World can add a low-stress introduction to theme parks by adding a Legoland visit before arriving in Disney World. Staying at the Legoland Hotel makes the visit even easier. And that is one of my favorite things about Legoland. It is easy.

CHAPTER FIVE

Wet Bricks at the Legoland Water Park

In addition to the theme park, there is a water park at Legoland. The first and perhaps most important thing to note about Legoland Water Park is that it is seasonal. Planning a trip in December or January with hopes of spending a full day in the water park is a sure recipe for disappointment. Deciding we wanted the option to do the Water Park made the decision to upgrade to an annual pass on our first visit easy. Our daughter may be part mermaid, as she loves the water, so it was not a surprise that when we came back months later to explore the water park, we had an awesome visit.

The Legoland Water Park is open roughly eight months per calendar year, opening in March and closing in October. Operating hours and even which days the water park is open vary, so it is always worth checking the current Legoland operating calendar on the Legoland website to make sure it will be open for your visit. It is also worth double checking tickets, as most but not all Legoland tickets will include admission to the water park when it is open.

In our eagerness to play in the water park, we visited near the beginning of the season in early March. So far, so good. Central Florida can be warm in March, so we thought we would be good on the weather. That worked out well. It was a nice warm day. Since it was a nice warm day rather than a hot summer morning, we spent the first part of the day playing in the park and riding rides. After lunch, we walked over to the water park.

Although our daughter was more or less done with strollers at this point, I went ahead and bought one for this trip. That gave us an easy way to pack in not only swim suits, but also extra dry clothes and towels. Unless something has changed since the last time we were at the Legoland water park, you are on your own for towels. I'd noticed this in a review on the water park but didn't quite believe it. As it turns out, that review was correct and I was very glad we brought towels. I also brought a small bottle of baby soap, as I prefer to shower as soon as possible after swimming to get the chemicals off. There is a large public bathroom at the entrance of the Water Park with shower facilities for those who want to rinse off.

There is no direct entry into the water park, so bringing these items required packing them all across the Legoland park into the water park that is positioned at the rear of the theme park. That was worth bringing the stroller. Paying attention to the other guests, I noticed that others brought in wagons for this purpose. If I was bringing a wagon into Legoland, I would want to bring one of the newer push style wagon. Being able to see where I was pushing the wagon reduces the odds I might accidentally run the wheels over some small child. I do not trust pull behind wagons in crowded public areas. It is difficult to control the steering on ours and I do not trust my own driving if I can't see what's going on.

Just past the Flying School roller coaster is the water park. A Lego mermaid water fountain guards the entry. When the park is open, guests come through this area into another gate area to scan tickets or passes for entry into the park. Once past this gate, there is a guest service area, shop and restaurant on the right and rest rooms and rental lockers on the left. The guest service area is where you can arrange to rent a cabana.

Cabana rentals start at $80 for the day and will vary by location and date of rental. We haven't indulged in a cabana rental yet, but if we ever plan a full summer day at the water park, I will consider that money well spent. A cabana rental includes the cabana with two lounges, chairs, a small fridge, safe, bottled water and a souvenir bag with complimentary towels in a cabana that can be closed for privacy or protection from Florida's summer afternoon rain and have a ceiling fan to keep the air moving on those room days. A host also comes by to check for and deliver food and drink orders from the Beach'n'Brick Grill. The grill offers typical park food including hot dogs, burgers, chicken nuggets and salads.

Guests are required to wear street clothing into and out of the water park. The rest rooms also provide changing areas and showers so that guests can switch into and out of swim gear. Adjacent to this are are the rental lockers. I highly recommend snagging one of these lockers. We usually get the largest size and stuff all our things in there so we don't have to worry about them while playing in the water parks.

The Legoland website has a great frequently asked question section for the water parks. When I went to check for the rental price of the cabana, I got sidetracked into looking at questions like does the water park have birthday party packages (no) and are water shoes allowed or required (required except for the water slides). I will keep an eye on this FAQ before our next visit to the water park and would suggest the same for anyone else thinking about a visit to the Legoland water park.

Once the three of us changed and applied lots of sunscreen, we secured what we needed to secure in the rental locker. Then it was time to go play in the water. My personal favorite in the Water Park is one of the very first attraction you see when entering the water park, the lazy river. Or, in Legoland terms, the Build A Raft River. This is a nice lazy river, with the addition of large, soft Lego bricks that can be built on the floats. All three of us love the lazy river and spend a lot of time in the water here. There are various Lego figures throughout the ride with water features, so any child who does not like water in their eyes may want to consider bringing goggles for this lazy river.

Next to the Build A Raft River is the Duplo Splash Safari. This very shallow pool features a couple of short slides and some oversized Duplo animals. Kids have fun turning wheels on these Duplo animals to turn water features on and off. The slides are a great way for kids to try waterslides for the first time or for kids who might not want to try the big slides for whatever reason. About half of the cabanas that can be rented are located by the Duplo Splash Safari.

Samantha's favorite water slide is either the baby slide at the pool at Disney's Kidani Village at the Animal Kingdom Lodge or the small slide at the pirate boat entrance to the big water slide at Storm Along Bay at Disney's Beach Club. These small slides at the Legoland water park are much the same concept. I might argue they are better, because there are multiple small slides at Legoland. In any event, it would be hard for Samantha to pick which she likes better, the lazy river or the little water slides.

Moving on into the park, there is the Build A Boat station. Here, kids can build personalized boats on Lego hulls, then send them racing against each other in a small water raceway. Samantha had a blast building a ship but she had absolutely zero interest in racing it, as she watched several other kids see their boats dash against the obstacles and break apart. She left her boat behind and moved on to the next water play area. I did not tell her that the Model Citizen watching the area took her boat apart as soon as it was clear she was done with it.

The Lego wave pool has minimal theming. It is a large wave pool. We enjoyed swimming in it and Samantha particularly liked practicing her floating skills here. We spent most of our time in the deep end, playing catch your child as she floated between us. I think we may have worried the lifeguards, as they paid a lot of attention to the three of us playing. That is likely a good thing, as there is no way for them to know how proficient (or not) guests are at swimming. I much prefer vigilant lifeguards because, well, you never know.

Samantha had no interest in the other two attractions in the water park. The three big water slides, known as the Splash Out, held no interest for her. She loves the baby slides and is unwilling to do basic slides, much less these giant multi-story drops. The Joker Soaker was also a no go due to random water drops. That's too bad, because I think she would have enjoyed the smallish water slides in this area if not for the random water drops and water spraying around. I think both these water attractions would be immense fun for kids—and adults—who enjoy either thrill rides or splash grounds.

Swimming is hungry play. One of the most reliable ways to get my water loving daughter out of the pool is to offer her food. We usually have snacks, as Legoland rules allow small coolers and snacks that do not need to be heated. Somehow though, those cheese sticks or yogurts never sound quite as good as a hot burger with fries or frozen treat. That is how we usually wind up adding a meal in the park to our plans. The grill at the front of the water park has the most options for food, although in reality it is a limited menu with burgers, dogs and nuggets for the most part. Two other food options include an ice cream stand and a street taco speciality shop. All park food options are overpriced for the quality in my opinion, per the usual theme park food inflation phenomena.

Going so early in the season, the water was fine but getting out was chilly. We spent maybe three hours in the water park that first visit before calling it good. Then it was back to the rented lockers to get our towels, dry clothes and other items. I was very glad to have that little bottle of soap so I could shower and shampoo before we left the water park. I also have to speculate that the park makes a reasonable amount of money from guests who do not know they have to bring their own towels. We saw a lot of people coming out of the gift store with new towels. Not one of them looked very happy about it.

While I was happy we took our waterpark bag in on the stroller, I was far happier to have the stroller to push with all our wet things in it rather than carrying that out by hand. Since we were all warm in our dry clothes, we did a couple of favorite rides before calling it a day and heading out of Legoland. If we had been packing our stuff out in backpacks or bags, we would have gone directly to the car to put it away. While going back into the park from the parking lot is easy, most of the time if I make it to the car, I'm leaving, so that would have cut this visit shorter.

Having the water park located inside the theme park is both nice, because you can play or ride the rides or see a show or whatever on the way in or out, and annoying, because if you don't have some easy way to carry wet things, that is a long walk out of the park.

I found that out the hard way on a solo trip later in the summer, when I came to the water park and floated on the lazy river by myself for almost two hours. The time relaxing in the water was awesome. Trudging back out of the park, hauling a backpack full of swim things was less fun.

Overall, perhaps it is for the best that the water park is a perk of the annual pass. To this date, the Legoland water park remains the only theme water park we have visited. One day, we'll get around to the water parks at Disney, SeaWorld and Universal Studios. Perhaps then I'll have an opinion on how they compare with each other. For now, I appreciate the bonus fun the Legoland water park represents to my family. Playing at the Legoland water park is a good way to have an awesome day.

CHAPTER SIX

Glamping Legoland

Our first few family trips to Legoland were a ton of fun. The simplicity of the park and the ease of going with the flow and doing whatever we wanted in the moment continued to be a nice change of pace from our other theme park adventures. Also, given just how much the park targets a certain age demographic, I wanted to be sure Samantha had plenty of time to enjoy the best of Legoland before she grew out of it. As it turns out, that window was far longer than I first anticipated. As Samantha has continued to be very interested in the Legoland park, I now think the window may go up to age 10 for many children.

In any event, towards the end of the school year, Samantha had a long school weekend, I had a vacation day and we had annual passes. We decided another trip to Legoland was well worth a few hours drive. However, budget concerns again ruled out another stay at the Legoland hotel. But we wanted to have more options for things to do than the Hampton provided. With camping very much on my mind as I'd just finished up my book on camping at Disney's Fort Wilderness, I went looking for camping options near Legoland.

It turns out that there are a lot of camping options in the area. For those who have RVs or are willing to tent camp, there are seven campgrounds to consider. As we wanted a cabin, that narrowed the search down to one, the Cypress Campground and RV park. This campground, located just over two miles from Legoland, had good reviews. I booked the one bedroom cabin for the weekend and we were off on another adventure.

In terms of cost, the one bedroom at the campground was around $100 per night. This was significantly less than the Legoland hotel, although obviously more than using points to stay for free at a chain hotel. One unexpected facet of campgrounds in this area was their busy season. Typically, the busy season in Orlando is connected to times when school is out. That's exactly the opposite for the Cypress Campground, as their business is tied to the snowbird set. The busy season for the campgrounds is the winter and the value season is the summer. For those looking for an extraordinary good value, you can rent a one bedroom, one bath cabin with a kitchen in this campground for less than $500 per week during the campground slow summer season of May through August. For comparison purposes, a summer week at the Legoland hotel may run around $2,500 and even the less expensive Beach Retreat is still nearly $2,000 for a week during the summer. Clearly, the campground cabin is a financial value.

We tend to spend time at a resort hotel, so amenities do matter to my family. Campgrounds often have a variety of activities for families. Cypress Campground offers a heated pool, clubhouse, horseshoe, shuffleboard, billiards, darts, laundry rooms, bathhouses, mini-golf, bocce ball, library, play area and a giant chess/checkers set. Those have been fairly typical of our experience at well reviewed private campgrounds, so that was about what I expected at Cypress. Unfortunately, some of these amenities had perhaps seen better days and were in somewhat disappointing shape during our visit. I hope the campground has since invested in some refurbishment, as it was past time to do some maintenance when we were there.

One additional amenity Cypress offers is unique in my camping experience. They have a private entrance to the adjacent Walmart. This is extremely convenient for campers with personal golf carts. In fact, it made me wish briefly that Cypress Campground offered golf carts for rent. I do love golf carts!

Realistically, the great value of the campground cabin included a few things that were not quite in line with my expectations of a resort stay. For example, the bed in the cabin was much smaller than I expected and the mattress was just this side of miserable. The bathroom was small yet fully functional so no issues there. Having a full size refrigerator, stove and kitchen sink is great for cooking easy meals, budget friendly meals while on vacation. The lack of a dishwasher meant my daughter had a rare opportunity to practice her dishwashing skills.

Again, for the cost, I still think this one bedroom cabin was a great value. We had a bedroom with a door and the small living room had a fold out couch perfect for Samantha's toddler bed. It is simply a caution that the level of comfort does vary with cost to some degree. I was so excited about the low cost that I had not stopped to consider that before booking this cabin.

Outside, the cabin included a picnic table on a concrete slab plus spots for two vehicles to park. Samantha had a blast blowing bubbles at this table one evening while we sat on the front porch sipping beverages.

The real estate people say it is all about location, location, location. From this point of view, Cypress Campground is a win. It is about two miles from Legoland, meaning you can be at the park within about five minutes if traffic cooperates. The campground is close enough to the park to easily get up, have breakfast and still make it to the park for the 9:30 early opening for annual passholders. It is also easy to then spend a morning playing, drive back to cabin for lunch and play time, while still allowing enough time make it back to Legoland for an afternoon show, rides and perhaps even fireworks before leaving again for the cabin for dinner.

That is the pattern we followed for two full days, the only variation being how long we stayed at Legoland versus the time spent checking out the mini-golf, swimming pool, play area and other amenities of the campground. It made for extremely relaxing days at Legoland. I would happily stay here at this campground again, but I would call first to see if they had upgraded the mattress before booking the cabin. On the other hand, if we ever buy the camper my husband has been talking about, we would stay here without a concern or second thought.

On our last day, we left early to stop by Disney World for some time at the Animal Kingdom and in Disney Springs. That worked out well, as this was on our way home. On the other hand, I would not want to plan to do a Disney trip while staying in Winter Haven. The drive is not too bad, but that's an hour and a half round trip that could be allocated to other important things, like napping, while on vacation. Ideally, if I was planning a first time visit to Legoland, I would book two nights at the Legoland hotel matched by two full days in the park. But if I wanted to manage my budget more tightly, either the Cypress Campground cabin or one of the local chain hotels would be the way to go.

CHAPTER SEVEN

Group Visits: Friends, Family & Kids

Sometimes, we talk friends or family into joining our adventures. This is a whole different level of fun. Well, and to be completely honest, a whole different level of planning. After many Legoland visits over a couple year period, Samantha, Craig, and I were old hands at the park. We can drift in and out to enjoy a couple of rides and chill for hours watching her play with Legos in different parts of the park. But when I'm playing tour guide and travel director for a larger group, my compulsive planning tends to kick in.

When considering group trips, I start thinking about things like: How many people or families are going to come? What day is everyone coming? Which hotel are we staying at? Has everyone made their reservations? Have you purchased tickets? Do you know which tickets to buy? Do you know where to get them? What rides to you really want to do? How do we make sure the kids get time to swim? Have you thought about bringing towels for the water park? All these questions and many more crowd into my head the moment one of my friends or family says "I think we would like to go to Orlando with you."

LEGOLAND WITH FRIENDS

Legoland is a great option for group trips for families with young children. The first group visit we did was with close friends who vacation with us every other year. This family—Kelly, John, and their three young children John, Ben and Elizabeth—have shared beach, camping, Disney and many other family vacations with us over the years. After listening to us talk about Legoland, they wanted to try a joint vacation that included time at the park. We made plans and decided on a trip with two days and a night at Legoland with these friends for their first visit.

So, what is really important to know about vacationing with friends who also have small kids at Legoland? Book the hotel. Don't overthink it and don't look to save money staying elsewhere. It isn't worth it. Just book a night or two in the Legoland hotel and the rest of the vacation will all but take care of itself. The kids will easily spend a couple hours exploring all the nooks and hidden treasures of the room. Then there is the awesome play area in the lobby. Plus the master builder class. And the pool full of floating Legos and all the other fun elements of the hotel designed for kids. And the Lego characters who meet fans in the hotel lobby. When all these entertainment options fail to keep the kids occupied, it is a very short walk into the park. The real win may be that short walk back to the hotel once the kids are worn out and naps are needed.

After listening to me go on in far too much detail, our friends agreed that the Legoland hotel sounded like a fine choice. Kelly booked a room at the Legoland hotel for their family. They have three small children, who at the time were seven, five and three. A family of five is the perfect size family for the Legoland Hotel rooms and the kids were arguably at the perfect ages to visit the Legoland park.

Of course, I didn't follow my own advice. Nope, while my friend Kelly was smart and booked her family at the Legoland Hotel, I decided this was the best occasion to try the Beach Retreat at Legoland. This is the second hotel for Legoland and is less than a mile from the park. It is less expensive than the Legoland Hotel and offers a slightly different set of amenities. I very much enjoyed the Beach Retreat and would happily stay there again with my husband and daughter on a future trip. However, staying in two different hotels made logistics of a joint trip far more complicated than necessary. On the positive side, all the kids got to experience the best of both resorts. On the negative side, it would have been less stressful for the parents to be an easy walk down the hall from friends rather than loading kids up and driving to a different place for meals, swimming or naps.

One other factor added some complexity to this particular trip. I was delighted that at the last minute, my mother in law took me up on a standing invitation to join us on vacation. I was delighted. She is an incredible lady whom I love and respect. However, I didn't really think through inviting Grandma to stay with us that night at Legoland Beach Retreat. I did a quick count of beds—three twins plus the king, so everyone would have a bed if Craig and I each took one of the twins in the children's alcove and gave Grandma the big bed. That seemed like it would work just fine and that is what we did.

Well, I must say that I will not do that again. Those twin beds are fine for kids. They are not comfortable for tall adults. I spent that night on the trundle bed, with the wheels gliding so effortlessly over the floor that the bed moved every time I moved. The next time Grandma comes with us, I'm getting a hotel room just for her. Or maybe a room for her and

Samantha to share while Craig and I have our own. You know, that option might be the best of all, now that I think about it.

We drove to and checked in at the Beach Retreat with no issues. Kelly and her family flew in to Orlando. She tells me it was an easy drive from the airport. Once they were close enough, we drove over to the lobby of the Legoland Hotel to meet them. As we all arrived later in the afternoon, we did not plan to do the park at all that first day. Instead,we first met up while they checked in. Our kids immediately all took off for the lobby play area to burn some energy. Kelly took care of checking her family in and visited with us downstairs while her husband John took the luggage up to their room. When he returned, we grabbed a table at the lobby bar by the play area and visited while the kids played. They were interested in the other hotel, so everyone decided to go have dinner at the Beach Retreat restaurant and play there for the evening. We rounded up the four kids, loaded them into the two vans and made that short drive back to the Beach Retreat.

The kids were still all wound up with lots of energy from the flight and drive. Going over to Beach Retreat was a good idea. The weather was perfect, so we walked around the resort, basically hopping from play area to play area. The rooms at the Beach Retreat are interesting. It is not like the traditional small hotel set up at the Legoland Hotel. Instead, these rooms are set up basically as duplexes circling around some point of interest, which is usually a play area. Each of the duplexes has two rooms and is designed to look like a bungalow built from Legos. They all have a small porch. If you think back to the very first house you built from Legos, these Beach Retreat bungalows likely look something like that. I like the look. It is a clever way to create some privacy and keep the overall noise level controllable in a resort built for kids.

The resort layout at Beach Retreat is great for families. The amenities, including the lake views, the play areas, the pool and the restaurant, are first class for what is basically a value resort. On the other hand, I think the room size is smaller than the Legoland Hotel. And some of the small touches, like the treasure hunt in the room and the master builder class, are missing from Beach Retreat. This is a fun resort for meandering, much like Art of Animation at Disney World. The whole resort is built on the lake, giving wonderful views. And all that outside space is great for kids to run around and play, at least when the weather is nice.

After checking out several different play areas and testing to see how close we would let them get to the lake, we had a pack of hungry children. The Beach Retreat restaurant is just as themed as you would expect from a Lego resort and included visits by Lego characters. The menu had a surprising number of options, but we kept it simple and opted for pizza for the kids. There is a play area inside the restaurant with legos and the only challenge we had was to peel the kids away from the toys long enough to eat. I don't really remember the pizza, so I assume it was fine. Instead, I remember the kids laughing and enjoying the chance to visit with our friends while the kids played.

After dinner, we stepped out to the large Beach Retreat pool so the youngest child, Elizabeth, could swim. She really wanted to play in a pool with giant Legos! The pool was more crowded than I expected but the lifeguards did a good job keeping an eye on everyone and keeping it fun. While Elizabeth enjoyed her dip in the pool, the older kids decided to go play some more. After watching Elizabeth swim and play with the giant soft Legos in the pool for a while, we went to join the big kids. Before our friends drove back to Legoland Hotel to check out their hotel room, we did several group photos. Beach Retreat is a joy for pictures. The bright primary colors and Lego decorations everywhere make it easy to get fun photos for remembering the trip. Setting up photos with the lake in the back is a bonus. If I had thought about it ahead of time or realized how well the Beach Retreat was designed for photos, I might have tried to arrange for a local photographer to meet us there to do some family photo sessions on vacation.

Once our friends got back to their room, they started the treasure hunt. I could all but hear the excited squeals a mile away. Yes, I mean that literally—I called when the three kids were working through the clues and there was a ton of excitement as they closed in on their goal. They finished up and opened the safe in time to get ready for bed and into pajamas. Once the nightly preparations to sleep were complete, John and Ben then talked their way into a little time in the kids section of the lobby for the pajama party. Their dad took them downstairs for a little more fun while their mom and Elizabeth crashed. The boys did not last long downstairs and as soon as the party ended, it was time to call it a day. Somehow, Elizabeth slept through her brothers climbing over her trundle bed to get in their bunks. I call that a win.

Our Beach Retreat room was fine. There was plenty of storage and a small fridge, which I really like in a hotel room. The alcove with the bunk beds was cleverly curtained off, which was nice. The bathroom was on the smaller size but fine for a short trip. One nice touch which we did not utilize was the outlets for charging devices on either side of the bed. I appreciated the counter space, as I think these rooms have more counter space than the Legoland Hotel. On the other hand, I missed the treasure hunt excitement. That alone might be a good reason for any first trip to be at the Legoland Hotel rather than the Beach Retreat. And, if you happen to have an extra adult along for the trip, Legoland Hotel has suites with more space and an extra bed.

The next morning, we were up early and had breakfast at the Beach Retreat hotel, which was included as part of our hotel stay. I enjoyed the breakfast more than the dinner the night before, although it was significantly more crowded. That makes sense, as breakfast is included with the room rate but other meals are not. I would guess that most families staying at Beach Retreat either eat dinner in the park or go out to one of the chain restaurants around Winter Haven. For that matter, if we go again, I might just order delivery pizza to eat at the table on the front porch of the bungalows and watch the kids play from our porch. They would probably stop playing long enough to come eat once they got hungry enough.

After breakfast, we gathered our things, checked out and made our way over to Legoland Hotel. Grandma did not want to visit the park, but she was comfortable hanging in the lobby while we visited. Our friends were not quite ready when we got there, so Samantha started off the day in the lobby play area. When our friends finished their breakfast, which was in the Legoland Hotel restaurant appropriately named Bricks, the kids joined her to play. That gave us adults a little bit to decide we would split up for the morning, with the moms taking the girls to the simpler rides while the dads took the boys on the thrill rides they wanted to enjoy.

Even with four children under seven, we did not bring strollers or use them at Legoland. Staying at the hotel meant even the youngest at age three was comfortable walking to and from the park. So with just the normal stop at security to check backpacks—while we didn't bring strollers, none of us were brave enough to tackle a park with kids without snacks and distractions—we were off to play in Legoland.

Craig tells me the boys all but raced to the back of the park to get to the Ninjago ride. They are big fans. The kids all loved this area. They did the ride, then took the time to play in the area in the courtyard of the ride. I don't have proof, but I think that Ben may have walked away with the high score on this ride, outdoing his big brother and both dads. Then the boys tackled the coasters, trying to get as many in as they could before meeting us for lunch.

On the other hand, Kelly and I took the girls to Duplo Valley. Samantha and Elizabeth played in the barn, then cycled through the different rides in this area. We tried to talk them into the spin ride or the coaster at the Castle, but that was a no-go. Instead, they did the Royal Joust before we walked over to the Friends area to catch one of their shows. We may have pushed it a little too far, because by the time our group caught up for lunch at the burger restaurant near Lego City, a couple of us were on the verge of hangry. Fortunately, some fast food ran off the hangry and we were ready for more Legoland adventure.

As the park allows small coolers, the next time we go with a group of small kids I might consider bringing in Smuckers Uncrustables and bag of chips for them for lunch. While it would be a cost savings, I think the bigger win is in the time saved. There are picnic tables in the park and pulling out a quick lunch would save both the time waiting in line to order and the time for the food to be prepared. With just a little coordination and luck on timing, one adult could easily go get food for the adults from one of the restaurants while the kids started their own lunch.

Well, with one appetite satisfied, the kids were ready to play again. We were right by the boats, so Kelly & John split the kids up in three boats while Craig and I watched, waved and took pictures. Next up was the Driving Academy. This ride offers Legoland Drivers Licences for kids. As you might expect, the dads had fun joking about those only being valid in the park.

Next up was the Imagination Zone. This pavilion houses a panini shop, several Lego play areas and the Mindstorm classes. Those are a lot of fun for older kids. Ours were not quite old enough this trip to have the attention span to enjoy Mindstorms. Perhaps we will do that on a future trip. Instead, John and Ben made their way directly to the racing area. These two competitive boys spent all their time in this area building cars to race each other. Both claimed to win each race, so I'm not really sure how that worked. They seemed happy in any event.

Samantha and Elizabeth went first checked out the digital playroom. They made electronic Lego fish, then set them free to swim in the wall sized digital aquarium. Elizabeth tired of this after making two fish and went to find something else to do. She found the flying station and spent the rest of her time building planes and sending them flying down the test line. Each flight made this girl giggle. I think she may have a future as either an engineer or a test pilot. Samantha tired of the digital fish too and went to find her dad in the earthquake area. They spent time trying to build structures that would survive the shaking.

Seeing everyone happily occupied, I walked over to the ice cream shop. Okay, I might have been thinking that kids and adults were going to need a bribe to get them out of that play area. I found a good bribe with a giant Lego brick filled with six scoops of ice cream and tons of sides. Bringing this back to the tables set up near the entrance to the play area and letting the other parents know about the ice cream got all our kids to the table to dig into the sweet treat.

Checking the time, we made our way back to the Legoland Hotel for the kids Master Builder class. One of the downsides to only booking one night at Legoland meant that by the time we checked in, all the evening Master Builder class times were full. Knowing how much Samantha enjoyed this from a prior visit, we went ahead and signed the kids up for an afternoon class. I think the class was around 4pm. Leaving for the Master Builder class mean the group only completed about half the rides and shows at Legoland in the time we were in the park.

The Master Builder class was the highlight of the visit. This really is one of the best things about a standout resort for kids. I love the classroom setting, complete with an overhead projection of what the Master Builder is doing that makes it easy for the kids to follow along with their blocks to replicate the build. Months later, we asked Elizabeth what she remembered about the trip. She smiled and started talking about the dragonfly she built and how much fun she had in the class. That's about the strongest recommendation I can give for signing kids up for the Master Builder class.

While the original plan had been to head back to the park after the class, the adults decided to split up and get us moving towards the next stop on this trip. Kelly stayed with the kids in the class. Craig, John and I visited with Grandma in the lobby. Once the kids finished class, we let them play in the lobby play area while the dads got the vans loaded and ready. Then it was time to load up and head towards our next adventure, SeaWorld. Excited about the time in Legoland, the older kids were able to stay awake for the drive. Both the younger kids dropped off for a nap before we left Legoland property. It's a lot of work to play hard in an awesome theme park!

It has been almost a year since this trip. When I touched base with my friend to see if she would ask her kids what they thought about Legoland, the response warmed my trip planning heart. John, her oldest, didn't miss a beat, saying he loved the hotel and asking when we would go back to play at Legoland again. His brother and sister agreed, leaving my poor friend to explain we don't have any plans to go back right now. I think they might still be trying to convince her to set a date for our next trip to Legoland.

LEGOLAND WITH FAMILY

One of the key takeaways from our trip with friends was that while one day might be plenty of time for us in Legoland, they would have enjoyed doing more than one day there. As we vacation with these friends regularly, we will probably get that extra time in on a future trip. Based on the feedback from our children, that trip will all but certainly be booked at one of the Legoland hotels and can't come soon enough.

On the other hand, when both my brothers and my dad shocked me by agreeing to spend Thanksgiving week in Orlando, I knew it was unlikely we would all be available to visit Legoland or any of the other parks in Orlando together again while the kids are all still young. Also, different members of the family want to do different activities while we are in the area. Some want to go to the Disney parks. Some want to go to SeaWorld. Some, honestly, just want to chill out without doing any of the parks. At least one brother is only coming because he wants to check out the new Star Wars attractions at Disney's Hollywood Studios. So we need a different plan for this trip.

I looked at the Legoland Hotel because I know my nieces and nephews would have a great experience there. However, price becomes an issue when looking at the five or more rooms per night it would take for us all to comfortably enjoy the experience. And since different families want to do different things, it just does not make sense to base our trip at Legoland. Instead, we are renting a large six bedroom house for this trip.

Did you notice I am talking about this trip in the future tense? That is deliberate—so far, we have planned this trip but we don't go for another few months. I will do a follow up post on the visit complete with pictures and tips on my website, www.ayearofdisney, for those would like to see how it turns out.

I am excited about this trip. Deciding to rent a house together means we will have the benefits of a large kitchen, game room, laundry and our own screened in private pool in addition to the play areas, pools and movie facility at the community where we are renting. Plus each adult or adult couple will have their own bedroom and the kids will have a separate space of their own. This will give us the ability to make and enjoy a traditional Thanksgiving meal together while on vacation. It should also give us the extra elbow room that makes family vacations that much more fun.

However, choosing to rent a home instead of staying at a resort close to the parks comes with some downsides. We will be giving up easy access to the different parks. Among other things, that means no returning to the room for an afternoon nap or rest or dip in the pool. I am also trying to prepare my family for the crowds that will be at the Disney parks this Thanksgiving. Thanksgiving 2019 is going to be the first major holiday that the new Star Wars themed land called Galaxy's Edge at Disney World will be open. That means it will be the first time many families with school age children can visit this new Star Wars land. I expect it to be an absolute madhouse. Wonderful and exciting, but crowded and crazy. By contrast, I am hoping that Legoland might be relatively calm. Since we are going to do Disney early in the week, spending Black Friday and Saturday at Legoland might feel even more awesome by comparison!

LEGOLAND FOR GROUPS: SCHOOL, CHURCH, YMCA, OR SCOUTS

While I have not been part of organizing or participating in a group trip to Legoland, I see these groups in the park frequently. That made me curious, so I started doing some research. I was impressed to discover that Legoland Florida has some great experiences and values for school groups. As I dug more into group possibilities, I discovered that not only does Legoland Florida have an impressive structure and curriculum around school field trips, they also have group options for church groups, YMCA groups and scout groups who might want to plan a visit to the park. In fact, the more I learn about these group possibilities, the more tempted I am to work with our church to try to get a group together to go visit in the future.

If you are considering pulling together a group visit, the Legoland website is the best resource for information. There are dedicated pages for school, church and scout groups. A little searching will give options to download PDFs with curriculum, map, logistics and welcome information. There is also a dedicated customer service group with its own toll free number (877-865-5346) to assist with questions and booking a trip. I called this group to ask questions to help write this section. Calling was a good experience, with the representatives able to answer questions and give suggestions. If I ever try to pull together a larger group visit, this number will temporarily go on speed dial.

Some of the advantages of a school field trip include cost, curriculum and some special learning experiences. The trips are available during the school year, which excludes July entirely as well as some days in June and August. These visits may only be scheduled Monday-Friday. The price, as of 2019, is $14.50 per student. This is an outstanding value in my opinion. No wonder I see school groups frequently visiting the park! That $14.50 per student includes admission to the park as well as the special educational experiences. A school group visit also includes one complimentary admission for chaperone per five students and additional chaperones can be added for less than $30 each.

Teachers can also download Educational Resource Guides that match the different Educational Experiences and include pre and post park visit activities to enhance student learning. While the water park is also available for an upgrade, I personally would not want to wrangle students in a water park. That just does not seem like fun to me.

The curriculum guides align to Florida standards and are available for grades K-6. This seems to indicate the school group visits are also for those ages and that makes sense to me. Legoland is a park built for kids and keeping the school groups targeted to elementary age matches that target demographic seems smart. While the curriculum is specifically reviewed for Florida standards, the school visits are open to schools from any state. If we were still living in Georgia, for example, I would already be talking to my daughter's teacher and offering to organize a trip for her class.

School groups are allowed to bring in coolers with lunches for the kids. The Legoland staff will help transport these coolers to and from the designated bus loading/unloading area—free parking for school buses is also part of the deal—to the area inside the park designated for school lunches. Other options include arranging lunches in the park restaurants, although this adds cost. One key point is that outside food delivery, like pizza for example, is not allowed in the park.

Reservations are required at least two weeks in advance. I don't know any teacher who would be willing to put something like this together with just two weeks notice, so my guess is the earlier you can plan the better. Also the website is clear that reservations are subject to availability and prices and offerings can change at any time. Payment for school trips is required at least 10 days in advance and must be arranged with only one form of payment.

Again, I really impressed by the pre-work Legoland had done to make planning a school visit simpler for educators. The relative value for the cost if your school is close enough for a same day visit seems impressive. One other offering that I did not know about is specifically for teachers. Florida teachers qualify for a free annual pass to Legoland. That truly is awesome.

While the Educational Experiences and $14.50 student prices are limited to school groups, there are other options for other groups. Qualified youth groups, such as YMCA, church youth groups, summer camps and scout programs can contact Legoland to set up a visit. These visits have a 15-child minimum at a cost of $29 per child and the same complimentary chaperone per five paid children offered to school groups. Further, groups participating in this program are also welcome to bring cooler lunches or arrange discounted lunches like the school groups.

There are two days a year designated as Scout Days in Legoland Florida, usually in May. These special days also feature planned activities for scouts and the opportunity to earn an exclusive patch. So now I'm thinking perhaps I should sign my daughter up for girl scouts after all with the not-so-secret agenda of getting her troop to take a trip to Legoland.

CHAPTER EIGHT

Beyond Florida: Legoland Discovery Centers

Unless you are a local or a family that strongly prefers a very relaxed touring style for theme parks, two full days at Legoland should be plenty to experience what the park and the water park can offer guests. However, if you are going to Legoland at all, odds are someone in the family is a Lego fan. In this case, it might be worth considering one of the annual pass options for the other attractions that come with these passes.

The current annual pass options for Legoland are the Awesomer Pass and the Awesomest Pass. Both passes include 365 days of admission to Legoland park and the water park, on days that the water park is open. Both passes include free regular parking at the park. The Awesomer Pass also includes admission to the Madame Tussard Wax Museum and SeaLife attractions at the iDrive 360 complex on International Drive. The Awesomest Pass includes admission to all Merlin attractions in the United States, including the Legoland Discovery Centers in Arizona, Atlanta, Boston, Chicago, Columbus, Dallas, Kansas City, Michigan, Philadelphia, Westchester and San Antonio.

The Awesomest Pass also includes the SeaLife aquariums in the US, several of which are either adjacent or close to the Legoland Discovery Centers. The

SeaLife aquariums are located in Arizona, Carlsbad, Charlotte, Dallas, Kansas City, Michigan, Minnesota, Orlando and San Antonio. If your travel budget and vacation tastes allow, you can also do coast to coast Legoland parks, as this Awesomest pass also includes entrance to the California Legoland and California Legoland and water park, albeit with some restricted dates. In 2020, the next Legoland resort opens in New York and it is possible the annual pass will cover this theme park as well.

This pass also covers some adult oriented entertainment in San Francisco. We have not visited the Dungeons, but they sound like fun. The website almost reads like it is an extended escape room with a little murder mystery tossed in, but we have not tried it so I don't know enough to have an opinion on this. If we make it to San Francisco while our pass is active, it might be worth a visit just to check it out.

LEGOLAND DISCOVERY CENTERS

On the other hand, we have visited two of the Legoland Discovery Centers. Both the one in Atlanta and the one in Dallas are great options for small taste of the Legoland park. Both of these Discovery Centers were located in reasonably large, upscale malls. Both offer a variety of activities, with some overlap and some unique. Both offer extras such as birthday parties, but the logistics and cost vary by location. And like the Legoland park in Florida, these Discovery Centers cater to school groups. Although I have not personally visited the other eight Discovery Centers (yet) it seems reasonable they would be built along the same lines. There is plenty to entertain a family for a half day visit at a Legoland Discovery Center.

We first visited the Atlanta Legoland Discovery Center. At the time, we lived a few hours away from

Atlanta and I had a work meeting there on Friday. My husband and daughter joined me on this trip for a weekend in the city. They spent all day Friday at the Discovery Center while I worked. That evening, my daughter was excited to tell me about their day at Legoland and very eager for me to go play there with her again the next day.

When we visited the Atlanta Discovery Center, all three of us had Awesomer Legoland annual passes that covered admission to this specific Discovery Center. That was a good thing, as my husband was as interested as my daughter in going back the next morning. They had fun playing tour guide, which is quite the reversal of roles in our family.

Discovery Centers are a mix of mini-lands, rides, theater and play areas. Visiting a Discovery Center might be a good way for a family to determine if they would enjoy a visit to the Legoland park. My brother did this for his family, taking them to the Atlanta Discovery Center. His family really enjoyed it and now plans to visit Legoland with us later this year.

Each Legoland park around the world and all the Legoland Discovery Centers feature a specific mini-land made of Legos. This mini-land is considered the heart of any Legoland. At the Discovery Center in Atlanta, the host city is recreated in miniature. And much like the other mini-lands, there are buttons to press that set off special effects such as moving characters or other items in the display. In much the same way, the 4D Cinema offers a very similar experience as the theater in Legoland. In fact, these theaters seem to offer the same short movies that we have seen play previously at the Legoland theme park in Florida.

There are two rides at the Atlanta Discovery Center. The first is Kingdom Quest. It is a smaller version of the Clutch Powers first person shooter at Legoland.

Guests board ride vehicles, designed to hold two in the front row and two in the rear row, and the ride takes off on a track in a dark room, with various goals for riders to shoot along the way. The Merlin's Apprentice ride is much like the Technicycle in the Florida park. This is a Dumbo style ride with vehicles radiating out in spokes from center point. However, guests provide the pedal power to make their vehicles rise. So parents, get ready for a work out, as the kids almost always seen to want to fly high on their parents pedaling.

The Lego factory tour takes you through how Legos are made. This is not available at the Legoland park and that's a shame. It would be a good addition, as this is a fun tour for any Lego fan. The Lego Master Builder Academy is much like the class at the Legoland hotel. Guests follow along with a Master Builder on a planned build. There are four distinct play areas at the Atlanta Legoland Discovery Center. One will be familiar to guests who have visited the Lego store in Disney Springs and built a small car to race down the track there. The Lego Racers is similar, with a somewhat larger track. The Duplo Village is a toddler's play area, while the Friends play area includes a karaoke component and may be more favored by slightly older children. The final play area is the Earthquake Zone, where guests build and cross their fingers their buildings last with the quake plates start shaking.

The Legoland Discovery Center in Atlanta also has a cafe, which offers basic sandwiches and snacks. Close to the cafe is the Birthday Party Room. For a fee, parents can arrange a Lego birthday party for up to 40 guests. Parties include admission to the Discovery Center, an hour in the birthday party room, with pizza and cupcakes for guests, and a private Legoland Master Builder class. Actually, this sounds like a lot of fun. If we lived in a city with a Discovery Center and wanted to invite to allowed 40 guests, then close to $600 price might be worth it. As is, I don't see us trying this anytime soon.

As my daughter's excited spinjitzu moves attest, the animated series about the Lego Ninjago world has created one of the most popular segments in the Lego universe. Characters from this popular storyline will return soon to the Atlanta Discovery Center. The theater will be showing a new 4D short movie featuring the ninjas—Loyd, Jay, Kai, Cole, Sane and Nya—from the Ninjago series. The Ninjago Training Camp will also allow kids to test their ninja skills in a play area that includes a laser maze and Ninjago themed building table.

Atlanta has a large play area built around a Lego pirate ship. Samantha played happily here for well over an hour and would have continued playing as long as we were willing to stay with her. As usual, the walk out means walking through a store. I don't know about you, but we have yet to walk through a Lego store without finding something to take home with us.

The other Legoland Discovery Center we have personally visited is in Dallas, Texas. This center happens to located right beside a SeaLife aquarium. Visiting the Discovery Center and the aquarium took us a full day. As expected, the mini-land depicted Dallas Fort Worth in Legos. This one is particularly fun. It is made from a million and a half Legos and includes some airships in flight. The Dallas Discovery Center has other attractions in common with the one in Atlanta, such as the 4D Cinema, Racers Build & Test, and the Factory Tour. Dallas also has the Merlin's Apprentice and Kingdom Quest rides. This location has an additional ride option for children, the Forest Ranger Pursuit. Kids climb into little cars and take off. This reminds me of the Driving School ride at Legoland Florida, albeit on a much smaller scale and themed differently.

The Dallas Legoland Discovery Center is slightly larger than the sister facility in Atlanta and includes a few additional attractions. My daughter's favorite was the Ninjago City Adventure. This is essentially a fun indoor ropes course for kids, themed to the popular Ninjago series. If your child is like mine, you already know about the spinjitzu from their antics copying the characters as they watch these animated adventures. This space is a great way to for them to play hard and expend some energy.

The Friends area is a little different. It is an opportunity to build in Heartlake City and take a selfie with the Friends. Or, if space is a stronger interest, you can build a spaceship in the Mission Space area. There is also a Duplo play area. Now, I understand that this is meant for the younger kids. But I actually still prefer playing with Duplos in a lot of ways. The pieces are much easier to handle and it is faster to build larger structures. Of course, that matters more when you are build a structure for a little one to knock down rather than building a more intricate structure for games and storytelling with an older child.

Outside the building, the Dallas Legoland Discovery Center has one more surprise. During the summer season, guests can change into swimsuits to enjoy the outdoor Pirate Beach. This splash area is full of water canons, slides and other water features. Much like other attractions reflect an attraction at Legoland Florida, this water area could be seen as a much miniaturized version of the Joker Soaker wet play area in the water park.

There are Legoland parks and Legoland Discovery Centers all across America. Legoland Florida is the largest of these and includes the largest variety of attractions. If your family is not sure if they would enjoy a visit to Legoland Florida, finding the closest

Legoland Discovery Center and spending some time there is a good indicator of how much the family may enjoy the park in Florida.

As it happens, we are planning a large family reunion in Orlando for Thanksgiving this year and are considering what type of Legoland tickets to get. I found a good deal for two day tickets at $85 per person for Legoland park only. That's fine, as the water park will be closed while we are there in November. But then I need to add in parking for two days, which is another $60. And while I don't think we will be back in the Orlando area to schedule another visit to Legoland or the water park, we live close enough to the Dallas Legoland Discovery Center & SeaLife Aquarium to visit these attractions multiple times per year. A discounted combo ticket for just the Dallas Discovery Center and SeaLife is $30, while an annual pass to these two attractions is $110. On the other hand, the top end annual pass at Legoland includes these attractions plus all the rest of the thirty plus Merlin attractions in the US for $199 per person. Between the planned Legoland Florida visit and a couple return trips to the Dallas Discovery Center, perhaps upgrading to the Legoland Awesomest Annual Pass makes sense for our family after all.

The Legoland Discovery Centers are certainly not full scale theme park. These are small spaces, usually within a mall, and feature a couple of scaled down rides, a theater and some play areas. That said, these are good for several hours of family fun and are easily accessible across the US, which makes this either a good bonus activity between Legoland visits or a relatively straightforward way for a family to inexpensively try a Discovery Center to see if they would enjoy a trip to one of the Legoland theme parks.

ORLANDO EYE 360 COMPLEX

Thinking about the Legoland Awesomest pass brings me back to Orlando and the two additional attractions you can visit if you choose to get that pass or the Awesomer Legoland Pass. Both of these pass options include access to the Florida Legoland theme & water parks, the Orlando SeaLife and Madame Tussauds wax museum as well as the Atlanta Legoland Discovery Center.

There is so much to do in Orlando that many families may not want to allocate the time to check out the two local attractions that come with the Legoland Awesomer pass. That was us, as it took a few visits before we got around to visiting these. The good news is that these attractions are much closer to the other big theme parks than the Legoland park. Both SeaLife and Madame Tussauds are located in the iDrive 360 complex on International Drive in Orlando, which is about 45 minutes from Legoland. However, this complex is only ten minutes from either Universal Studios or SeaWorld if you get lucky with traffic on International Drive. Again, depending on traffic, the iDrive 360 complex is perhaps 30 minutes from Disney World. There may be some irony in the fact that I first visited the iDrive 360 complex to use my free admission from the Legoland annual pass while on a trip to visit SeaWorld.

The good news is that once you brave the traffic on International Drive, finding the iDrive 360 complex is easy. Just look up for the giant sky wheel. There is a garage with complimentary parking right beside the complex. After parking head down the elevator or stairs and walk a few steps to the entrance. Once inside the skywheel building, the wax museum is on your left. On the right is the aquarium. Straight ahead is the entrance to the skywheel. Prior to 2018, the skywheel was also included in the Legoland annual

Awesomer pass. However, the skywheel recently changed ownership and is no longer included with either Legoland pass.

It is really too bad the skywheel is no longer part of the Legoland annual pass program. That is my favorite attraction at the iDrive 360 complex. The first time I went was on a solo trip to check it out and see if my family would enjoy doing these attractions. I got really lucky with timing and managed to go up for the first time at sunset. Watching the sun set over Orlando from the Eye was fantastic. One of the items still on my bucket list is an adults only couples trip to Orlando with my husband, which will include a ride on the Eye at sunset with the upgrade for a private ride vehicle and champagne flight.

I mentioned much earlier in this book that one way to avoid parking fees at Legoland would be to take the shuttle from this complex down to the park. We have not done this, as I'd rather drive myself to have control of when and where we go. It is possible I have control issues. In any event, if we were staying at one of the International Drive resorts or perhaps even SeaWorld or Universal Studios and wanted to go to Legoland for the day, this shuttle would be a decent option. As a bonus, the wax museum and aquarium are typically open later than Legoland, so there would be more to do if anyone in the family had the energy after a day in the park. On the positive side, there are far more dining options on International Drive than around Legoland, so perhaps planning this and ending the day with a nice dinner would be fun and more relaxing than driving to Legoland and back from this part of town.

Looking back, I was far more confused than I should have been for my first visit to iDrive 360. Once I booked my hotel on International Drive, I called the skywheel customer service number to ask about visiting these attractions using my pass. That call turned into one of those frustrating customer service experiences where I stare at my phone after hanging up, wondering why I bothered to call at all. The most helpful information the customer service representative gave me was "just show up. We will work you in." I don't know about you, but that is not very reassuring to me when I am trying to get actual information.

None of the materials for annual passholders included directions or much at all on the iDrive attractions. Not knowing what to do, I was glad this first visit was a solo trip. After all, if I was going to make a fool of myself, it was much better to do so in front of perfect strangers. Plus, it makes the experience better for my family if I have a good handle on the logistics. This may be a logical corollary to the fact that I like tourist attractions far more than my husband does, so the easier I make it, the more likely he is to go along with my interest in visiting these attractions.

In any event, once I found the place and parked, my first stop was at the counter for the skywheel. It took a bit of discussion at the ticket counter, but eventually we figured out that I could have skipped that step and gone directly to the ticket holder line. Okay. Sometimes I make things more complicated than they really are.

Once I got in the right line, my pass was scanned, I went through security and the obligatory photo opportunity and was directed to the waiting deck. This is just another queue area, with a slide presentation that includes interesting trivia about the skywheel. When the doors open, they lead to a theater that shows a father and daughter riding the skywheel around Orlando attractions before ending in space. When this show ending and the doors on the other side opened into a bar, I wondered just who did that bit of strategic planning. Later, I learned I could easily skip this whole experience and go directly from the photo op to the outside loading queue for the ride. Unless you really want to see the movie, save some time and go directly to the ride.

The outside final waiting area has a nice view of the capsules as they slowly approach and depart the continuous waiting area. Stepping in and out is easy, as the ride moves in slow motion about about one mile per hour. It is not a short ride, as it takes about twenty minutes for one full rotation. Each of the capsules are climate controlled and hold up to fifteen people. Well, that is what the occupancy sticker suggested. Fifteen people on one of these would make for a crowded ride. Fortunately, in the half dozen or so times we have gone, the most I have ever seen in one capsule was six people. That is perfectly comfortable.

The view changes during on time of year, time of day and weather. And as interest level changes from person to person so widely, the capsules also have iPads with information on the different things you can see. That's a nice touch. That very first ride, I was lucky enough to catch the view right around sunset. That is a lovely view. In fact, it was enough to think that on a future adults-only trip, perhaps Craig and I should spring for the upgrade to a private ride with the champagne option. If you are lucky enough to bring grandparents, nanny, au pair or other responsible adult who can be convinced to take your exhausted children back to the hotel after a day at Legoland, finishing out the evening with a ride with your significant other on the skywheel might be reason enough to park at the iDrive 360 complex and take the shuttle to Legoland for a day trip.

After exiting the skywheel, next up on my agenda was a visit to Madame Tussauds. This was my first visit to a wax museum and I was not really sure what to expect. What I did not expect was difficulty getting into the attraction. Having figured out that I was supposed to be in the ticket holder line, I waited there for my turn. It was a very short wait of perhaps a couple minutes at most. When I presented my annual pass, the gentleman at the entrance desk said it would not work. He knew it was supposed to work but said the computer systems did not communicate well. He suggested that I go wait in a different line to get a new pass printed and then return.

That suggestion did not work for me, perhaps in part because I had tried to get this kind of information ahead of time unsuccessfully and also because I had started the visit at the main desk trying to make sure I had everything I needed without a return trip. I rather firmly suggested that we find some alternative to me waiting in a different line, as we both understood my pass was legitimate for entrance. To his credit, the gentleman found another way. He gave me a comp ticket of some kind. Actually, they didn't scan anything. I think he decided it was not worth it and just waved me through.

This is perhaps my one real beef with Merlin Entertainments and it continues to this day. If you are going to create, market, and sell annual passes with access to multiple attractions, make it work for all those attractions. Don't promise your guests one thing then make it hard for them to use what they paid to use. I get that not many guests will take advantage of all the attractions included in the pass. That doesn't matter. If it is part of the pass, make it work for the guests.

Last month, after finding conflicting information on different Merlin Entertainment websites about current annual pass options, I decided we should go ahead and get our annual passes now in order to visit the SeaLife and Legoland Discovery Center in Dallas rather than putting off a visit there until after our planned November Legoland trip. Several places stated this was possible, but clicking on links to purchase tickets only led to the Florida or California park sites.

Much like the gentleman at the Florida wax museum, the customer service manager who happened to be standing in line at SeaLife to direct guests was very helpful in trying to make something that should have been easy work. He worked with me for almost two hours to try to find a way for me to purchase that annual pass through his system. He even sent my family into the attraction as a courtesy while we tried to make it work. Ultimately, we could not find a way. So I purchased annual passes to Legoland Florida online on my phone while this gentleman watched. He issued us separate courtesy annual passes just for the Dallas attractions as the system literally could not print the annual passes I had just purchased. That was kind and I appreciated it. However, he truly went to the next level of service by personally emailing Legoland Florida to explain what happened and try to make it easy for us to pick up our passes there when we visit that park.

I deeply appreciate this level of customer service. It is the kind of going above and beyond on a personal, individual level that makes me happy to support the Legoland parks and attractions. But it also strikes me as disrespectful to the employees and guests who have to go to these lengths to make something that really should be as easy as possible—spending money to buy a ticket—a true logistical challenge. I have this vague hope that perhaps this book will ultimately wind up on the reading list of some Merlin executive who will have the authority to either get the system fixed or change it so that it is not a problem. After all, everyone needs a dream.

Going back to the wax museum in Orlando, I enjoyed walking through the exhibits. There is a tribute to Walt Disney that struck me as particularly appropriate given the location in Orlando. Learning more about how wax molds were made was fascinating. And perhaps the most intriguing part of the visit was realizing that I am taller than many movie stars and other famous people. That was actually quite startling, as I expected these stars to be much taller than me.

I think older kids and teenagers would enjoy the wax museum. There's not as much for younger children. When we took Samantha on subsequent visits, she more or less raced through the wax museum exhibits in her hurry to get done and get to the real attraction for her—the aquarium.

After the difficulties with the annual pass admission at Madame Tussauds, I was a little skittish about the aquarium. But I really wanted to walk through it as well so that I would know if my daughter would enjoy it or if we should skip time the iDrive attractions to spend more time doing other things while on vacation in Orlando. Spending the extra time at the aquarium was well worth it. There were no issues with the pass. I enjoyed the short introduction video.

The aquarium is small and very well done for the size. In fact, it almost seems sized to be a child's favorite play area. There are interactive games throughout the exhibits. Kids can get a small book with spots to emboss after learning more about different animals and ecosystems through the aquarium. Even the tanks are as interesting as the animals they hold, as there are many different sized and shaped tanks for kids to crawl under, through or around. The tanks have different view ports, so children can pop up and look inside. This makes for great photos, except the prohibition on flash photography favors videos over photographs.

There is even a play area towards the end of the aquarium for kids as well as the requisite touch tank. This is always a hit for my daughter when we visit any aquarium. She loves reaching out and touching the animals. And of course, this then takes you into the store which concludes the attraction.

I enjoyed most of my solo visit here. Going first meant I was very comfortable with the logistics on the next trip when Craig and Samantha and I went back together. As far as family visits, Samantha loves the skywheel and the aquarium. This is a low key attraction that is a nice counter to the hustle and bustle of the busy theme parks in Orlando. And, well, especially on warm August days, it is nice to have a climate controlled option that will make the whole family happy. While the iDrive 360 complex will never be a top priority for us on trips to Orlando, it is nice to fit in a visit on occasion.

CHAPTER NINE

The Past: Cypress Gardens

During our first visit to Legoland Florida, I was some-what surprised to see a botanical garden on the park map. While there are some cute Lego flowers and trees, these two things are not really a natural fit in my mind. A quick google search revealed that the land currently occupied by the Legoland Florida theme park has a fascinating history. The Legoland garden is a small piece of the original park to inhabit these lands over eighty years ago. The more I learn about this past, the more it intrigues me. Long before Mickey Mouse, Harry Potter or Shamu came to live in Florida, there was a park in Winter Haven named Cypress Gardens.

The Cypress Gardens park opened in January of 1936 as the brainchild Dick Pope and his wife Julie as a botanical garden with plantings from all over the world. There is a story that Pope came up with the idea after his wife showed him an article from a Good Housekeeping magazine about a Charleston home owner who opened his gardens to the public for a fee. The park originally was a showcase for some 8,000 varieties of flowers planted along canals on the banks of Lake Eloise.

Cypress Gardens remained a family business focused on the garden and lake attractions until 1985. During this time, necessity was often the mother of invention. Today, you will see Lego Southern Belles in the Cypress Garden section of Legoland Florida. This is a nod to decades of hoop-wearing employees who decorated the park. This tradition and park trademark began one day in 1940 when Julie Pope realized a winter freeze had killed some of the garden vines. She asked employees to dress in period dress with large skirts to hide the damage. Just a few years later, Julie Pope displayed this same sense of action when some soldiers asked her when the water ski show would begin. The story goes that knowing both that there was no water ski show and that her children could easily show off some of their tricks, she named a time that afternoon and made it happen. The water ski show was very popular with the soldiers. When several hundred soldiers visited the park the next weekend, the water ski shy became a staple of the park. Legoland Florida continues this tradition with a daily water ski show.

The late 1940s, 1950s and 1960s were good years for Cypress Gardens. Hollywood producers used the Gardens as settings for movies, TV shows and commercials. The Popes continued to be heavily involved in promoting Cypress Gardens and Florida for tourism. One of the lasting changes to the park created for one of these movies is the Florida pool. This pool was built in the shape of the state of Florida on the lake and is currently open to the public as part of Legoland. The film industry industry was good to Cypress Gardens, creating revenue and interest in the park. Some sources claim that at one point in the 1960s, Cypress Gardens was the second most visited attraction in the United States, trailing only the Grand Canyon in number of visitors per year.

While the Pope family was publically very supportive of Walt Disney's investment in a new theme park in Florida in the 1960s and 1970s, the new theme parks steadily drew visitors away from Cypress Gardens. In the early 1980s, Dick and his wife retired, handing the business to their son. Not long after inheriting responsibility for Cypress Gardens, Dick Pope Jr sold the property to the conglomerate known at the time as Harcourt Brace Jovanovich (HBJ) in 1985.

The next few decades would see the park change hands several times, as different groups tried to make the park successful again. Successive ownership saw the focus move from botanical gardens and lake water ski shows to amusement park rides to compete with the other theme parks in the area. From 1985 to 1989, HBJ invested in new park attractions before selling the property to Busch Entertainment Corporation. A few years later, Busch Entertainment sold Cypress Gardens to the park's own management team. The economic and tourism slump that followed 9/11 in the United States ended Cypress Gardens in 2003 when the park management announced its closure. Wild Adventures theme park reopened the park in December of 2004 with the addition of four roller coasters and many other amusement park rides. This version of the park also struggled and ultimately failed in 2008, with the park closure announced in 2009.

In January 2010, Merlin Entertainment announced the purchase of Cypress Gardens as the location for their fifth Legoland park. This announcement brought tentative hope that Cypress Gardens might have found an owner that could bring sustainable new life to the park. The new Legoland park opened in October 2011. In the years since, Merlin has poured resources into the park with the addition of several new themed lands and two resort hotels. I believe that Merlin Entertainments has a solid strategy with ongoing investment that is setting Legoland Florida up for long term success.

While the nods to the park's past with the Lego Southern Belles, water ski shows and incorporation of prior amusement park rides strike me as appropriate and even respectful, it is the methodical step-by-step approach of turning this park into an overnight destination that I think is going to lead to Legoland Florida's long term success. Creating a park that brings joy and can be successful over the long term seems to me to be the very best way Legoland Florida can honor the rich history of its location.

While it is certainly possible to enjoy Legoland Florida without setting foot in the gardens that preserve the original park, it seemed fitting to pay tribute to the past here. All of the information in this chapter is distilled from internet research, which I have tried to verify with multiple reputable sources. Some of the best resources are the books Images of America: Cypress Gardens and Cypress Gardens, America's Tropical Wonderland. For a high level overview of this information, check out The Expedition Theme Park channel on youTube. It has a great video titled The Closed History of Cypress Gardens—Florida's First Theme Park. This video, which is featured in the Expedition Extinct playlist, includes some great period video and images from the park's long history.

CHAPTER TEN

The Future: Pirates, Matey

Opening as a new theme park less than 10 months after acquiring Cypress Gardens, Legoland Florida has seen steady growth since opening late in 2011. In 2012, the park opened the water park, which was a smart move capitalizing on the existing infrastructure from a prior water park attempt. The water park opening was followed by the new theme lands of the World of Chima, Heartlake City, Ninjago World and the repurposing of the World of Chima into Lego Movie World. These park improvements added capacity and provided new guest experiences.

I believe the biggest impediment to Legoland's long term success is the location of the park. Back in the early days of Cypress Gardens, the park benefited from location as the state highway was the major transportation line in the region before I-4. Now, the distance from the interstate is a challenge. One way to overcome that challenge was to turn the park into a multi-day experience. Adding and improving the park attractions gives guests a reason to visit or continue visiting the park. Creating highly themed hotels on the property that fit the park—the park designed for kids—is moving Legoland to a destination worth a couple of days of vacation time.

The clearest example of this so far might be Movie Land. With the new Lego Movie Land, Legoland partnered with Warner Bros. to invest in an immersive themed land with a characters and landscape the target audience will recognize and appreciate. In order to make a tighter connection between the hotel and the new land, the rooms previously themed to pirates have been redesigned to match the Lego Movie Land. This change gives the park the opportunity to do something different with the pirate theme. Recently, Legoland announced they are taking on pirates in a big way. Legoland is building a third hotel, which essentially duplicates the first Legoland Hotel, based around a Pirate theme. This new hotel is scheduled for completion in a much shorter timeframe than the first hotel, with an announced opening in the spring of 2020.

Before the new Pirate Hotel opens, there are rumors of a new miniature golf course for hotel guests opening in the summer of 2019. I expect this to be located near the Legoland Hotel and will be curious to see if Beach Retreat hotel guests are also invited to play miniature golf.

While I am not aware of any other announcements at Legoland Florida, a brand new park opens in New York in 2020. With three Legoland parks in the United States plus five more around the world, popular new attractions can be replicated throughout the system. Well, at least in theory I would expect to see this kind of synergy. As Legoland Florida is the second largest park in the system already and has the benefit of additional land for expansions, I look forward to what the future holds for the park.

With this rate of expansion, I can see us making at least one trip a year to Legoland until my daughter loses interest in the park when she hits her teenage years. I am very much looking forward to booking one of the new rooms at the Pirate themed hotel when it opens.

Acknowledgments

As always, thank you to my husband, daughter and mother-in-law for the time to write these books. However, as one person is more responsible than anyone else for my interest in Legoland, I want to do a special call out to her. Cyndi Daniels took her grandson, who is roughly the same age as my daughter, to Legoland for his birthday. Then she came back with stories about how much her grandson and the whole family loved the park. Cyndi, this book's for you, because you started this whole thing! Kelly & John, thanks for joining us on vacation at Legoland and letting me use stories from the trip in the book. I can't wait till our next trip together. And thank you to Bob at Theme Park Press, for the extreme patience with this book.

If you have enjoyed these stories, I invite you to join us at ayearofdisney.com and A Year of Disney on YouTube for more tips, tricks and adventures. Let's all go have some fun!

About the Author

I'm Amy and I love Disney World. It is a source of fascination, delight, and a momentary escape from the complexities of the real world. Who doesn't enjoy the thought of good conquering evil and happily-ever-after endings?

Back in the real world, we live in Savannah, Georgia. My husband and I are raising our daughter to share our love of imagination and stories. We love to travel and learn new things. My day job is an endlessly fascinating challenge, as it relates to why people do things in the workplace.

One reader got in touch with me after finishing my first book, *A Year of Disney* (Theme Park Press, 2015), to suggest that I post photos or videos from the different trips to give them some context. I was happy to point him to the Year of Disney YouTube channel, where you can find tons of videos from our trips. If you enjoy Disney videos, odds are you'll find something to enjoy at YouTube.com/ayearofdisney.

For Disney photos, swing by Facebook.com/yearofdisney, where I post a new Disney photo several times each week. For more on the books and our adventures, plus information on some of the other things we enjoy at Disney that don't fit into the books, check out some of the short blogs I have posted at AYearOfDisney.com. And if there is anything that you would like to see covered in a future book or video or article, don't be shy! Email me at ayearofdisney@gmail.com and let me know.

About Theme Park Press

Theme Park Press publishes books primarily about the Disney company, its history, culture, films, animation, and theme parks, as well as theme parks in general.

Our authors include noted historians, animators, Imagineers, and experts in the theme park industry.

We also publish many books by first-time authors, with topics ranging from fiction to theme park guides.

And we're always looking for new talent. If you'd like to write for us, or if you're interested in the many other titles in our catalog, please visit:

www.ThemeParkPress.com

• •

Theme Park Press Newsletter

Subscribe to our free email newsletter and enjoy:

- ♦ Free book downloads and giveaways
- ♦ Access to excerpts from our many books
- ♦ Announcements of forthcoming releases
- ♦ Exclusive additional content and chapters
- ♦ And more good stuff available nowhere else

To subscribe, visit www.ThemeParkPress.com, or send email to newsletter@themeparkpress.com.

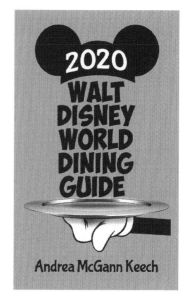

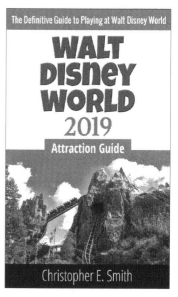

Read more about these books
and our many other titles at:

www.ThemeParkPress.com

Made in the USA
Columbia, SC
25 April 2021